Sefer HaMidot

The Book of Character

Rabbi **Nachman** of Breslov

נחל נובע מקור חכמה

There is no known book without mistakes. Therefore, I ask in every language of application if anyone has any questions, comments, clarifications, corrections, please send to: **book@simchatchaim.com**

All material used in this section may not be used for commercial purposes, but only for study and teaching.

To get this book or books and information Email me at:

book@simchatchaim.com

Copyright©All Rights Reserved to

www.simchatchaim.com

YB"S©All rights reserved to the Editor

First Edition 2023

Sefer HaMidot

The Book of Character

CONTENTS

3.	Introduction	102.	Forger
9.	Second Introduction	103.	Ancestral Merit
15.	Lost Article	103.	Memory
15.	Love	104.	The Elderly
16.	Eating	105.	Zeal
19.	Widower	105.	Novelties of Torah
20.	Faith	107.	Marriage
27.	Truth	108.	Dream
32.	Land of Israel	109.	Favor
33.	Clothes	110.	Flattery
35.	Shame	111.	Investigation
39.	Trust	111.	Nature
41.	House	111.	Purity
43.	Crying	113.	Wandering
43.	Children	113.	Lineage
56.	Blessing	113.	Fear of God
56.	Tiding	116.	Salvation
57.	Arrogance	118.	Honor
60.	Theft	121.	Sorcery
62.	Judge	121.	Anger
63.	Cognizance	124.	Learning
69.	Travel	135.	Mockery
71.	Instruction	136.	Slander
72.	Hospitality	138.	Circumciser
73	Sweetening of Judgements	138.	Money
		150.	Informer
84.	Success	150.	Famous
86.	Thoughts	151.	Miscarriage
94.	Distancing the Wicked	152.	Contention
		165.	Messiah
96.	Pregnancy	165.	Beverages
97.	Seclusion	165.	Music
97.	High Position	166.	Menstrual Impurity
102.	Confession	167.	Deriving Benefit from Others
102.	Defers		

Sefer HaMidot

168.	Sexual Immorality	195.	Righteous
175.	Foul language	217.	Charity
176.	Test	225.	Spiritual Impurity
176.	Trial	227.	Curse
178.	Memorial Lamp	228.	Jealousy
178.	Auspicious Action or Object	229.	Nocturnal Emission
179.	Secret	230.	Difficulty in Childbirth
179.	The Counting of the Omer	231.	Vision
		233.	Mercy
180.	Book	234.	Healing
181.	Redeeming Prisoners	235.	Oath
		235.	Sabbath
183.	Codifiers of the Law	236.	Bribery
184.	Fear	236.	Slaughterer
187.	Abstinence	237.	Sleep
187.	Sin	237.	Drunkenness
187.	Punishment	239.	Peace
188.	Brazenness	240.	Joy
189.	Humility	242.	Officials
191.	Depression	243.	Chastisement
194.	Advice	245.	Prayer
195.	Constipation	254.	Repentance
195.	Laziness		

2

Sefer HaMidot

Introduction

This book elucidates all the traits and conduct arranged according to the aleph-bet/alphabet. It is divided into two sections which are known to us by the names "Aleph-Bet of Old" and "Aleph-Bet of New." The first part is a wondrous collection, collected by our pure and holy master in his childhood, all that his huge intellect perceived by understanding one matter from another; and he gathered from all the holy books, everything that he found in them pertaining to morals, conduct, and upright behavior - which he recorded to have by him for memory's sake. Whatever he found elucidated in the words of Our Sages of blessed memory, whether it be a virtue of a good trait, or the opposite - derision of a bad trait - everything in its entirety he would gather little by little and copy them by him in the order of the Aleph Bet by each and every trait, so that he should have them for remembrance, to see with his eyes the significance of each and every trait and its converse, in order to go in the ways of the good and guard the ways of the tzaddikim (based on Prov. 2:20). Moreover, his powerful intellect perceived many precious and wondrous matters which are not explicitly elucidated in the words of Our Sages OB"M; just by the sheer magnitude of his perception he understood one matter from another, and conceived precious novelty in the concepts of the traits from within the Scriptures and from within the words of Our Sages OB"M, which are not explicitly elucidated in their words, just hinted to - for a genius of his caliber.

Everything he gathered and assembled together in the order of the Aleph Bet, and in the course of time there was found by him a complete compilation on all the traits, and he instructed to copy all of it, and from his mouth he read to me, and I transcribed in the book (according to Jer. 36:18), in order that this book should not desist from our mouths (Josh. 1:8) to speak and think it always, in order that we cease from

Sefer HaMidot

bad traits. For everyone, when he sees arranged the utter derision of a bad trait and the great loss it causes, and the dreadful violation that is realized through it, he will have compassion on his soul, and he will gird his loins to stand up against it, and he will beseech from He to whom mercy is His, to escape with his soul from the abyss, to save him from those bad traits or bad desires or similar ones, and so in the converse regarding good traits.

Furthermore, (Prov. 16:20 - Rashi) one who gives heart to contemplate his words (to forge his way), will find good - true advice how to guard one's self from any particular vice, through making sure to be safe from the vice which is close (in the set up of the book, and it thus revealed that they are associated) to, for they are neighbors to each other, and each one guards her friend, as (this is) explained subsequently in the introduction that I heard from his holy mouth. The importance of this book, there is no need to explain, to anyone honest, who desires truth, and longs with cherishing to grasp the ways of propriety, certainly he will find in it a repose for his soul. Fortunate is he who takes hold of it, then it will be good for him in this (world) and in the coming (world), because this entire book is founded on verses of the Bible (Torah, Prophets, Scriptures) and on the words of Our Sages OB"M, all of them cogent to the understanding and straight, for those who have found cognizance (Proverbs 8:9).

The second part is also similar to the first part, in form and arrangement, there is no (marked) difference between them, for it is also an elucidation of the virtue of good traits and the derision of bad traits and the like.

Nevertheless, there is a difference between them, for the items elucidated in the first part, on each and every trait, they are matters which are elucidated in the holy books, explicitly or at least in allusion, so that someone who puts his heart to understand the matter, and who he who wants to study in

Sefer HaMidot

depth to understand one matter from another, can understand and comprehend from where the Rav extracted this item, from which verse or from which teaching of Our Sages OB"M. For, all the matters elucidated in the Aleph Bet of Old are not remote and not distant (based on Deuteronomy 30:11) from the one studying them - to come to its property, to understand and comprehend from where the items effuses. Albeit, without the Rav, who illuminated our eyes with these matters, it would not have occurred to the reader to extract these matters from within the holy books. However, after he already opened our eyes to these matters, it is possible for the enlightened (reader), whose heart is complete with the holy books; with the Tanakh (acronym for: Bible, Prophets, Scriptures - 24 books in all), and with the Aggadot (lore) of Our Sages OB"M, and with the other commentaries, to understand and comprehend the relevant sources.

In contrast to this, the issues elucidated in the second part are lofty and awesome conceptions perceived by the author OB"M, in the days of his greatness. All of these matters transcend human comprehension and are hidden from all eyes. For each and every item there is a very wondrous and awesome taam (reason, taste, cantillation, secret) and it is supported by some verse or teaching of Our Sages OB"M through a very wondrous and fabulous allusion, in his wondrous style, as the reader will see for himself. For there are many items elucidated here without (presentation of) any reason or proof, and within the major compilation of discourses (Likutay Moharan - A Collection of the Teachings of Rabbi Nachman) it is expatiated there, a complete matter, and a wondrous and awesome exposition on this item at great length, and this you will find in many places. So too one should learn the characteristics of the vague from what is explained, that also in the places that he did not explain the item explicitly, also there his masterful hand attained a complete conception of it (the item presented without elaboration), just, for some ulterior reason he did not want to provide the explanation of the item.

Sefer HaMidot

For all these matters, all of them are supernal and from a holy place they traverse, from a very extremely awesome lofty source, and they do not contain a single matter which does not command an awesome and wondrous exposition on what its foundations were cast, the reason for the matter, its characteristics, and a very hidden, deep, and wondrous support from within the Written Torah or Oral Torah. It is not for us to elongate on the paramount praise of these matters, because all who add, detract. For it is not hidden from our eyes the lowliness of our worth - and the greatness of our master the holy Rav, supernal candelabra, OB"M, and his utter hiddenness and concealment from the eyes of the world (people), this being the case, we must put restraint to our mouth, to be silent and not to mention, not to relate the magnitude of his holy praise, not a matter nor half a matter, and the enlightened will be silent now, Almighty G-d Hashem - He knows and Israel will know (based on Joshua 22:22). Fortunate is he who waits and reaches the days that have aspiration, at the time when the glory of Israel will rise, truth from the earth will rise (Psalms 85:12), a language of truth will be established forever (Proverbs 12:19), it does not say 'was established' but 'will be established' (Tikunay Zohar 63, pg. 95a). The medication for the matter - silence, everyone, according to the fathoms of his heart, will understand and comprehend the extent, to where these matters reach.

Still, we come with these words, to arouse the hearts of the readers, to make known to them the nature of the book and its affairs. It is incumbent upon us to make known and reveal to the ears of our peers (the hasidim of Breslov), that our honorable master, the hidden light, of holy and blessed memory, warned strongly to engage in this book, and that it should not cease from our mouths, for it is our life. He himself wrote it in a very small volume and said that his intent was to enable each and every one to carry it with him always, because the traits are the foundation of the entire

Sefer HaMidot

Torah - and with this a youth (or someone of that standing) will make his ways meritorious to heed everything that his written in this book, then he will bring success to his ways, and then he will be enlightened. For this is the main task of a person, all the days of his life, to flee from vice and bad desires, and to cling to virtue and upright conduct, that are elucidated in this book.

Fortunate is the person who listens to these words, to fulfill all that is written herein. He will never slip (based on Psalms 112:6) and his righteousness will answer for him in the time to come (based on Beraishis 30:33), when he comes to receive his reward. In the measure that a person meets out - so (In that same measure) is he met with. Fortunate is one who chooses life - Hashem will repay his endeavors, if it is to scoffers He will scoff (Proverbs 3:34), he will not gain wealth and his wealth will not endure (Job 15:29), woe to his soul - for the retribution of his handiwork will be done to him (Isaiah 3:11), it will not be cast to the ground (but on their heads -Job 15:29), one who is good before G-d will escape from it (Ecclesiastes 7:26). How great is the goodness hidden away for him (based on Psalms 31:20), in his joy no stranger will take part (Proverbs 14:10), a laboring soul benefits from its labor (Proverbs 16:26, see also Tractate Sanhedrin 99b - he works here and his Torah works for him elsewhere). Let us pour out our souls to Hashem to put our portion with Him, to stand at the threshold of His shade, they will have no regrets - those who put their trust in Him (Psalms end of Chapter 34), no eye has seen (their reward) except for You G-d, what He will do for those who put their hope in Him (Isaiah 64:3).

The words of the transcriber, whom is reduced to sighing and is crushed by the departure of the splendor of our heads, the majesty of our strength, the cherishing of our eyes, what can we say? May G-d (lit. the place - for G-d is the place of the world and not vice versa) comfort us very soon, the little one, Nussun, son of my master my father our teacher Rav Naftoli

Sefer HaMidot

Hertz may his candle shine, from the greater Nemerov, son-in-law of the Rav, the genius, the famous, the tzadik, our teacher Rav Dovid Tzvi OB"M Chief of the Court of the Congregation of Muehluv.

Sefer HaMidot

Second Introduction

Now behold, this holy book had already been published once, and since it is cherished there was high demand, and there is not even one copy remaining. For many are the people who desire this book, that in such a compact volume includes all the traits as we as many other matters, and much advice to reach straight paths in serving the Creator. There is nothing in the world that you are deficient in, that this book does not address, as the reader will see with his own eyes. It is all founded on mountains of holiness, verses from the Bible, Prophets, and Scriptures, and the words of our Sages, may their memory be for blessing, in the Talmud, the Midrashim, the Zoharand the other holy books. Thus, we decided to print the book a second time, with many emendations and wondrous, new additions.

This is to make known, that this book I transcribed letter by letter from his holy mouth. For by him OB"M, he had written - on small pages, all these things and more - possibly even twice as much. But because he did not desire to give over all of his words - which he had by him - written in a fashion similar to this, therefore he did not want to hand over his manuscript to me the way it was, to copy it. Rather, he attended to this personally, his honorable self. He read before me with his holy mouth, word for word, from within his writings (mentioned above), from his mouth he dictated to me, and I wrote in the book. It was heard from his mouth, that he said, that on the entry (lit. letter) of "healing" alone, he had many many pages written, it seems that he said - two hundred pages, but he did not want to give them over to the world.

Also, I heard from his holy mouth, that he told over before me, a long time before he gave over to me this Alphabet Book to transcribe, that he had by him certain writings on all the traits, and other matters - and they are the words of this book. He then (continued and) told me that he had perceived all the healings in the world (encoded) within the divisions of the

Sefer HaMidot

Land of Israel described in the book of Joshua. For the names of all the cities which are written there along the dividing lines of the country, are permutations of the names of all the medications in the world, how they are called in all the languages. For, the Land of Israel is a complete spiritual structure, and the apportionment of the Land of Israel is according to the structure of man, that is that this section and border is the aspect of the head, and this section and border is the aspect of the right hand, and similarly all the twelve borders of the Land of Israel, which was apportioned to the tribes, all of them are according to the arrangement of the parts of the human structure, as this (concept) is brought down in the holy books. He (Rabbi Nachman) said, that by every border of the Land of Israel, there is written there the medical treatment necessary for that limb, which corresponds to this border, as explained above.

All of this I already heard from his holy mouth, and I understood from his holy words that he attained all these understandings in his very childhood. But we did not merit to receive from him only what is written in this book, that which he looked and saw and weighed the matters with his holy intelligence, what should be given over to the world - which is the material he gave over to be copied as mentioned above, and what was necessary to hide from the world, that he deemed to have burned (as is described elsewhere).

Now behold, by him OB"M, there was written all these matters that are in this book with citations to the places from which he extrapolated these perceptions. However, when I copied them down from the dictation of his holy mouth, he gave me only to copy these things as they are, and he did not say where the sources were. But from the inference of his holy words, I understood that any man can find some sort of source or allusion for these items, from where they effuse, from which verse or adage of our Sages OB"M. Some of them are explicit adages in the words of our Sages OB"M, as the reader can see with his eyes. Several people have already

Sefer HaMidot

toiled on many matters from this book and found where they are alluded to.

Now, as we work on printing it a second time, I was moved in spirit not to copy from these allusions and sources, not a full matter nor half a matter, for many reasons, and also because we still did not do justice to find allusions to all the matters, therefore mind was set not to present any of them. However, afterwards I reconsidered, for just because one cannot complete a mitzvah etc. (does that mean he should not do it at all?) everything that is in one's power to do, one should do. Therefore, I decided to present several sources for parts of the work that I or my peers had already found, an allusion as a source, where there is a hint to the matter at hand in the Torah; written or oral, and a meager few that I heard from his holy mouth, personally, as will be elucidated in its place. For there are many things that are written here in brevity, and in reality, he revealed on those matters a lengthy Torah (discourse) with wondrous and awesome explanation, in his extremely wondrous style.

One who looks with truth will understand on his own, that after all this, even in the cases where we found the hint, it is just that, a hint and a support, but the actual substance of the issue, in the way he perceived it, is hidden from our eyes, for all his words are the words of the Living G-d, that he attained perception of each and every matter in the place that he perceived, and the verse is just an extraneous support, for there is nothing that isn't hinted to in the Torah, therefore if he did not draw up the shards and remove the mask of blindness which hovers over our eyes, and reveal to us these perceptions, we would not find the jewel, because it is not in our power to adjudicate and learn out by ourselves such things from verses and words of our Sages OB"M, only someone who merits to really sanctify himself until he merits to attain perception from above (is capable of such), and he who is wise will understand all of this on his own.

Sefer HaMidot

Also, I revised the format for these holy teachings, for the first Aleph-Bet book was published not in my presence, and the printer messed up, because he printed the second Aleph-Bet by itself and put it completely separate from the first one. This is not the way I would have it done. For even thought they are different in many ways as explained above, even still they should not be distanced one from another, since the both of them are good, and both address the nature of the traits, their virtues and their faults etc., certainly it is fitting to present together all the material relating to one trait. Such as the letter Aleph - Emess (Truth), it is proper and appropriate to compile together the material relating to the virtue of honesty and the derision of falsehood, even though the perceptions if the second Aleph-Bet very vastly surpass and surmount those of the first, as mentioned above, even still their inner intent are the aimed at the same thing, to reveal the derision of falsehood and the virtue of honesty in order that we strengthen ourselves with all our might not to speak dishonestly, just the truth in the name of G-d. It was for this that he revealed to us all the advantages achieved through honesty, and the converse, all the losses which come about through falsehood, and in what way one merits to truth, and so forth. So, it is with these matters - if their sources, where they were carved from, the places from which they effuse, are different one from another, for higher and higher is the guard etc (Ecclesiastes 5:7), even still they are all return to one place, so that we should merit to truth.

Therefore, I decided to present everything in order, so that everything together would be complete in one arrangement according to the alphabet. Just - I drew a line between the items of the first Aleph-Bet and the perceptions of the second Aleph-Bet, and I presented the second Aleph-Bet in small letters, in order for the reader to know to differentiate between it and the first Aleph-Bet. For I have already disclosed, that I heard from his holy mouth, that his his later words - those of the second Aleph-Bet greatly and vastly surpass and surmount the first ones, therefore I put a border

Sefer HaMidot

between them, to differentiate and to distinguish.

The good Lord should lead us in the straight and true path, so that we may merit to learn and teach, observe, do and fulfill all these words written here, and to understand and comprehend all the paths of advice elucidated here next to each trait. Then we will have success in our way, and then we will be enlightened.

It should also be noted that many items of the second Aleph-Bet are found repeated. The reason for this is, for know brother, that the second book our master OB"M gave over to us in his holy handwriting, and by him the material was not written in alphabetical order, just in order of the perceptions, according to what he perceived each and every item in its place and time, but he instructed us to copy the material and arrange them, each and every item, according to the trait associated to it, in alphabetical order. He also charged us, explicitly, that everything that is relevant to two or three entries, that we should write them two or three times - (once) by every (applicable) trait, and so we did. For example, in the letter Lamed - Limud (learning,book two, item #4): Someone whose Torah learning etc. that his eating etc. through this his enemies are judged etc., this item is pertinent to (the entry) Limud -Learning, and also related to Meriva - Conflict, and also relevant to letter Aleph - Achila - Eating, therefore it is written in all these places. From this learn out to the rest. For his holy intention was to facilitate for the reader, who desires to sanctify himself, to find what he seeks with ease. So that if he wants to know the segula (what is auspicious for) and the idea of any trait, he will be able to find with ease, according to the alphabetical arrangement, any matter that comes to his mind. As in the example above; sometimes a person wants to search to find a concept of learning, and sometimes he wants to find from a concept of holy eating etc., therefore it is worthy that it should be written in both places in order that he be able to find what he is looking for with ease, in the place that he is interested in, and so forth with the other traits. For this reason, the items are repeated in many places.

The blessed G-d should lead us in the truthful path, and just as we merited to arrange them so we should merit to fulfill them, until Israel returns to their habitat like doves to their windows, very soon, in our days, amen, so should be the Divine will.

Sefer HaMidot

Sefer HaMidot

Lost Article

1. Someone who returns a lost article to its owner, with this strength he makes converts.

Love

Part I
1. When there is no love between people, they go about gossiping. Through gossip, they come to mockery, and through mockery, they speak falsehood.

2. Through hatred comes upheaval, and through hatred come fires. lit: things get burned.

3. Through the love of the Lord, may He be blessed, the soul is guarded from all evil calamities.

4. If you first repent from your sins, you can come to love of the Lord, Blessed be He.

5. One who prays with self-sacrifice for the people of Israel is loved by all.

6. Through love, one is strengthened.

7. If you strengthen a person in his service of GOD, blessed-be-He, he will love you.

8. Through saying Hallelin a loud voice, one merits to love of GOD, blessed-be-He.

9. If you will be careful to avoid needless hatred, then when you have a legal case with a strongman who isn't willing to settle with you, through this he will settle with you.

Sefer HaMidot

10. One who is careful to avoid making a false oath, he certainly will not transgress the commandments not to take revenge and not to bear a grudge.

11. Garlic is conducive [segula] to love.

12. One who serves out of love - his merit protects for two thousand generations.

13. In the place where an agreement or a covenant is made, the Lord, blessed is He, is present there.

Part II
1. When plants grow to completeness, through this there is love in the world.

2. The love of a woman for her husband can be discerned by the flies and mosquitoes in the house. Also, through their love, it is possible to know the power of the evil inclination, whether it has been weakened or not.

3. Sages of the generation with love between them, that they see each other occasionally, then they have the power to judge the whole world, and their judgment stands, and no one can change or annul their judgment, for the Holy One Blessed be He is their Supreme Judge of their court.

4. Through needless hatred, one comes to eat non-kosher food.

5. Through lust of eating, one comes to love one of his sons more than the others.

Eating

Part I
1. From what you eat, leave over, so that GOD's blessing may imbue your food.

Sefer HaMidot

2. A man's proper conduct at his table purifies him from all his sins.

3. A man's proper conduct at his table merits him the World to Come, and merits livelihood, and that he is inscribed for good in the highest heights; and it merits him additional strength and might at the time he needs it.

4. Due to the sin of procrastinating justice, and distorting, and ruining judgment, and for neglect of Torah study, drought comes, and people eat without being satiated, and they eat their bread in measured rations.

5. When one eats a little, he is [lit. his heart is] drawn more after food than one who has not eaten at all and has already given up on eating.

6. Why did the Jews become liable to annihilation? Because
they took part in the feast of that evil one [Achashverosh, in the story of Purim].

7. The Altar of the Holy Temple dispels evil decrees, atones sins, nourishes and gives love. And the table [on which one eats] is similar to the Altar.

8. One who eats without first washing his hands [in the way prescribed by halacha] is as if he had relations with a prostitute. And one who trivializes the ritual hand-washing is uprooted from the world.

9. One should not drink water in public.

Part II
1. One who [manifests] the Image of GOD, through eating something that had life [like meat or fish] elevates it [/he himself is elevated], and so the reverse - [one without that Image degrades that food/ himself].

Sefer HaMidot

2. Eating fish arouses sexual desire.

3. By saying Birkat HaMazon [the grace after the meal], the Blessed GOD becomes known in the world.

4. By saying Birkat HaMazon [grace after meal], the government is settled from strife and wars.

5. One who learns Torah with a clear mind, that his eating is so holy that he is nourished from the [same] food from which the angels are nourished, causes that his enemies be punished with strangulation. This is learned from Torah passages: "And it was on the third day, when it became morning…", "And in the morning there was a layer of dew…" "And it was in the watch of the morning…"

6. One who does not taste anything when he eats, should know that the Blessed GOD has separated Himself from him.

7. The eating of tzaddik im is higher than the sacrifices, and higher than their conjugal relations.

8. The fish are fat in the merit of the sacrifices.

9. One who was bitten by a dog, it is certain that the mercies of Heaven are removed from him, and it is also certain that he has erred with eating forbidden foods.

10. One who guards himself from forbidden foods, he is saved from wild animals.

11. One whose enemies are on the rise; he falls into the desires of food.

12. Through desires of food, one comes to love one of his children more than the others.

13. "Come eat my food [bread] and drink……." - the initials of the Hebrew words in this verse spell Lulav [palm branch taken on Succos]. "...with wine..." with the four letters of the word, has the same gematria [numerical value] as the initials of Etrog, Hadas, Arava [citron, myrtle, willow]. [The word] "Masachti -I mixed..." - is an aspect of Sukkot [in that the words share the same root letters]. [Thus, we derive that] through the mitzvah of taking the Four Species and through [dwelling in] the Sukkah, a man merits to have food, drink, and clothing, and also that his soul will receive life-force. Through the sukkah one merits to have clothing, an aspect of "When I placed clouds as his garment." Through the willow one merits drinking, through the myrtle one merits to vitalize the soul, and through the lulav and the etrog one merits eating, for they have fruits, which are types of food.

14. **Food** and drink come through law and justice.

15. **That** when a man drinks, he begins to sing and play music, which is not so with eating, is because they sang [praise to GOD] about the [miraculous] well, but they did not say songs of praise about the manna.

Widower

Part I
1. **One** whose wife has died should recite daily the Torah passage describing the Guilt Offering [Usham], until he marries a different woman [This can be found in the Book of Vayikra, Chapters 5 and 7].

Part II
1.**Through** falsehood, one's words are not heard. Also, through falsehood, one becomes a widower GOD forbid, from several women.

2.**When** a man's wife dies, it is as if he is missing one of his bones. But the tzaddik, even though his wife passed away, he is not deficient a bone. This is [hinted at in the word], the

Sefer HaMidot

acronym for: "Not one of them is broken." [a'chas m'ayhem l'oe n'ishbara].

Faith

Part I

1. It is necessary to believe in Hashem, may He be Blessed, by way of faith and not by way of proof.

2. Through humility, you merit faith.

3. When you see something unusual happen, do not say it happened by chance. Rather, believe that this is the providence of Hashem, may He be Blessed.

4. There are things that cause great damage to the world. This is a difficult matter - why were they created, You should know that, certainly, they have one good aspect in them.

5. Someone who enjoys the words of a heretic, even if the words are not heretical, through this, he comes to thoughts of idol worship.

6. Through faith, a person is beloved to Hashem, may He be Blessed, as a wife is to her husband.

7. Someone who does not prepare his heart, is not able to come to faith.

8. Someone who has lost something, it is certain that he fell from his faith.

9. Someone who lost his faith, should go to Jewish graves and tell over the loving-kindnesses that the Holy One, Blessed be He, did for him.

10. Faith depends on a person's mouth.

Sefer HaMidot

11. Through learning Torah, all the heresies are broken.

12. Through faith, one is blessed.

13. Through excessive eating, we fall from faith.

14. When you gaze at the skies when they are clear and bright, you merit faith in the sages.

15. When some difficulty about Hashem, may He be Blessed, befalls you, then be silent. Through the silence, your thoughts will themselves provide you the answer to your question [See also Likutay Moharan vol. 2, Torah 7].

16. When they insult you, and you remain silent, you merit to understand an answer to your problem, and you merit the spirit of understanding.

17. When a person has learned and very wealthy opposers, know that this happened because he fell many times from faith.

18. Faith is considered like charity.

19. Through faith, one become wise.

20. At first, one needs to believe in Hashem, may He be Blessed, and afterwards, he merits to understand Him intellectually.

21. The mating of the Holy One, Blessed be He, is through the souls of Israel.

22. A person's intentional sin brings heresy in to a person.

23. When one falls from his faith, he will weep.

24. Faith comes through silence.

Sefer HaMidot

25. Through jealousy, a person falls from his faith.

26. Someone who does not have faith, it is certain that he belittles words of Torah.

27. Someone who is constantly cleaning his hands, through this, he cleans his heart.

28. When a person falls from faith, he should know that they are judging him Above.

29. When one falls from his faith, he comes into the grip of an accidental emission, into the grip of thoughts of women, and into the grip of idolatrous thoughts.

30. Faith comes through charity.

31. Through faith, it is possible to understand Hashem, may He be Blessed.

32. Through faith, it is possible to come to trust.

33. Through faith, the Holy One Blessed be He will forgive you for all of your sins.

34. Sometimes, the Holy One Blessed be He sends suffering to a person and smites him, but does not cast him down into weakness. This is only for the sake of faith.

35. Through a false oath, one falls from faith.

36. Someone who lacks faith does not accept moral criticism.

37. Someone who does not believe in the words of the Tzadik, ultimately, he will have no benefit from the matter, even thought he sees [the matter come to pass].

38. Someone who lacks faith, it is certain that the decrees of the Holy One Blessed be He are despised by him.

39. The Messiah will come quite suddenly. As a result, because of joy, Israel will be frightened.

40. When the Messiah comes, then all the ministers above and below will get sick. But now, when a minister ascends, Israel are sickened.

41. In the time to come, each one who is younger in years than his fellow, will be higher [See also Rabbi Nachman's Story Tales of Ancient Times, the Story of the Seven Beggars, the story of the blind beggar and what is explained there].

42. Jerusalem was only destroyed because they profaned the Sabbath, nullified the recital of the Shema in the morning and evening, nullified [the Torah learning and prayer of the] young children [tinokos shel bais rabban], were not ashamed one from another, made the small and the great equal, and also did not rebuke each other, [and] also humiliated Torah scholars, [and] also men of faith desisted from her.

43. Jerusalem will only be redeemed through charity.

44. War is the beginning of the redemption.

45. Someone who raises pigs, he holds back the redemption.

46. Jerusalem will not be rebuilt until there is peace among Israel.

47. The fact that Israel goes in exile from nation to nation is a sign that the Messiah will come.

48. When the nations exceedingly disgrace us, this is a sign of the Messiah.

Sefer HaMidot

49. The Holy Temple will not be built until arrogance ceases [See also Likutay Moharan Torah 57].

50. Through the unity that will exist in Israel, the Messiah will come.

51. The Messiah will come in a year of blessing.

52. The Messiah will not come until all the souls have left the [supernal] body.

53. Someone who marries off his daughter to a Torah scholar, gives him to benefit from his wealth, and does business for a Torah scholar, merits the Resurrection of the Dead.

54. Someone who marries off his daughter to a Torah scholar, gives him to benefit from his wealth, and does business for a Torah scholar, merits the Resurrection of the Dead.

55. Someone who is a man of truth, he can recognize in another person if the other person speaks truth or not.

56. Falsehood - the majority will not agree to upon it.

57. The Holy One Blessed be He hates the man who says one thing with his mouth and other in his heart.

58. A deceitful wealthy person [who denies having the possessions of others] - the mind cannot bear him. He is also despised in his own eyes.

59. To repair the mouth - give charity.

60. Through truth, the world is protected from all damages.

61. Through adulation, one comes to falsehood.

Sefer HaMidot

62. Someone who gives charity - his reward is that he will merit truth.

63. Through falsehood, you will certainly hate the humble.

64. A person can be recognized through his servants whether he loves falsehood or not.

65. When there is no truth, there is no kindness.

66. When you have falsehood, when the Holy One Blessed be He wants to perform some salvation for you, then the falsehood reveals your sins, so that He will not save you.

67. Through truth, the Holy One Blessed be He redeems you from all suffering.

68. Better for a person to die, then to live and be considered a liar in the peoples' eyes.

Part II

1. Sometimes, a person comes to a certain place, and he suffers in that place. He should know that his forefathers were in this place, and some heresy befell them. Or, his children will come at this place to some heresy. Because of this, he bears suffering now in this place.

2. Through adulation, one comes to heresy.

3. The Holy One Blessed be He does not perform wonders except for one who believes in two worlds.

4. Through faith, the decrees that the nations decree upon us are nullified.

5. Know, that each and every grass has a specific power to heal some specific sickness. This is only for someone who not does not guard his faith and his [organ of the] covenant,

Sefer HaMidot

and does not guard himself from transgressing "do not disdain anyone". But someone who has perfect faith, and he also guards his organ of the covenant and fulfills "do not disdain anyone", his healing does not depend on types of grasses which are specific to his illness. Rather, he is healed by all food and drink, in the aspect of "He will bless your bread...", and he does not need to wait until they provide specific grasses for his healing.

6. The main salvation which is coming, is only through faith. And the attribute of faith is according to the leaders of the generation.

7. When one goes from master to master, then he needs to strengthen his faith in the Unity of Hashem, may He be Blessed. Because learning from many teachers damages faith in the Unity. So too, the master who has faith in the Unity, he is able to illuminate to each and every student according to his ability, and each student only hears what he needs, and no more.

8. Consolation comes through faith.

9. Through the diminishment of faith, flies increase in the world.

10. Someone who guards himself from transgressing "do not covet", through this, he is saved from anger and arrogance and from a lack of faith which comes through anger and arrogance.

11. By not making GOD liness known to the nations of the world, through this, the nations of the world incite and seduce Israel to follow superficial sciences.

12. Through spoiling of faith, judgments are aroused. And through thoughts of idol worship, judgments of judgments are aroused. That is, they judge the judgments that were judged already, as to whether they were judged properly and without leniency.

13. Bereavement of children comes, GOD forbid, to someone who cast down his fellow from faith.

14. A woman who is careful about challah [piece taken from dough] - her children are faithful.

15. Through faith, the mind is settled.

16. Through Torah one comes to faith, and through faith, one comes to sanctify Hashem.

17. Someone who is not able to sleep, should arouse in his thought faith in the Resurrection of the Dead.

18. Those of little faith - it is difficult for them to conceive original Torah ideas.

Truth

Part I
1. One who wants to attach himself to the Blessed GOD, to the extent that he can traverse with his thoughts from heichal to heichal [chamber to chamber], and to see the heichalos [chambers] with the eyes of intellect, must guard himself from saying falsehood, even by mistake.

2. It is permissible to alter the truth for the sake of peace.

3. Those who are included in the grouping of liars cannot receive the Divine Presence.

4. It is permissible for the tzadikim to act with conniving with a swindler.

5. All who add, detract.

Sefer HaMidot

6. Through falsehood come thoughts of idolatry.

7. Through truth, one will not die before his allotted time.

8. From the breath [of the mouth] of a liar, the evil inclination is created, and when the Messiah comes, [then] there will be no falsehood. Consequently, there will be no evil inclination in the world.

9. Someone who is a person of truth then he can discern in another, whether the other is lying or not.

10. The indication of falsehood - when the many do not agree with it. It is one of the three things that the Holy One Blessed be He hates.

11. A rich man who denies that he is holding onto someone else's money - the conscience cannot bear it, and he becomes despicable in his own eyes.

12. A rectification for the mouth - that he should give charity [It is interesting to note that in the Hebrew alphabet the letter Peh - mouth, is followed by the letter Tzadik - the aspect of charity].

13. Through truth, the world is protected from all harm.

14. Through adulation, one comes to falsehood.

15. One who gives charity his reward is that he will merit to truth.

16. A liar hates humility.

17. A person is recognized through his servants, whether he loves falsehood, for each is dependent on the other. Sometimes his servants fall into sin through that which he is a liar, and sometimes he falls into falsehood through his servants, that aren't proper.

18. When there is no truth, there is no kindness, also he cannot do [kindness] with people.

19. Falsehood forestalls salvation, for falsehood exposes one's sins, in order that he not be saved.

20. The truth redeems from all troubles.

21. It is better for a man to die, than to live and be considered a deceiver in peoples' eyes.

22. When there is truth, there is peace.

23. Someone who is far from truth is far from charity.

24. Through truth, the sign of the covenant, [referring primarily to sexual purity] is guarded.

25. Through truth, one merits to an everlasting name.

26. A husband and wife who are accustomed to saying lies, their children will be opposers, and also will violators of the covenant [referring primarily to sexual infractions].

27. Falsehood comes through accepting upon one's self fear of people.

28. Through falsehood, one forgets the Holy One, Blessed be He.

29. Someone who does not have trust in GOD, he speaks lies, and through his falsehood, he cannot have real trust.

30. According to one's distance from truth, so one perceives a person who shuns evil as a fool.

Sefer HaMidot

31. One who wants to turn away from evil, and sees that there is no truth in the world, makes himself as a fool [because the world doesn't recognize the truth, they will see his turning away from evil as foolery].

32. Someone who does not lie, the Holy One Blessed be He saves him in the time of his trouble. Also, he will have children.

33. Through pointless speech [/lies - the Hebrew word "shuv" can mean either. The emphasis of this word is on open and blatant falsehood], comes a smiting of the children.

34. One who is connected to aimlessness comes to forgetfulness.

35. Through falsehood one comes to promiscuity, and strengthens the hand of evildoers, not to repent.

36. Through falsehood, one will not be able to receive healing, even from many varied treatments.

37. One who speaks falsehood [the emphasis of this type of falsehood -'kuzuv' is not honoring an agreement]. falls by the sword, also he becomes a fool.

38. Through fear of GOD, one comes to truth.

39. One who guards himself from falsehood, he is always victorious.

40. It is permissible to alter the truth in order to save oneself.

41. One who loves falsehood, he disgraces the Tzaddik, and he also becomes disgraced.

42. One who speaks falsehood, he is lost or destroyed.

43. Through truth, one is guarded from evil speech lushon hura, and his prayer is accepted. Also, when he is judged above, he is judged according to his merits.

44. Through dreams, a person can know if his heart is true with his GOD.

45. Someone who keeps his word can be enterprising make things happen.

46. Someone who doesn't have arrogance is saved from falsehood.

47. Someone who guards himself laughter of ridicule, it is certain that he is a person of truth.

48. One who was a liar in a previous incarnation, through this, when he was reincarnated, he was made to be left-handed.

49. One who guards himself and speaks truth at all times, it is as if he made the heavens and earth, and the sea and all that is in them.

50. Falsehood is only with one's mouth, but not in writing.

51. The Torah, the Prophets and the Sages spoke in the vernacular.

Part II
1. Through falsehood, one's words are not heard. Also, through falsehood, several women can become widowed, GOD forbid.

2. Through truth, His unity is revealed in the world.

3. When you see a liar, know that the leader of this person is also a liar.

4. Through falsehood, one comes to sexual immorality and spilling of blood, and also causes the upright people to fail in sexual immorality and spilling blood, and he shows permissibility from the Torah.

5. Someone who does not alter the truth with his words [the terminology here is used frequently in the context of not honoring one's commitments], he is able to humble the high and raise up the lowly [This concept of humbling the high and raising the low is found also in the Story Tales of Ancient Times that Rabbi Nachman revealed, in the 4th story of the King Who Decreed Apostasy - the King's great success came from a statue that had certain powers which were contingent on the King raising the low and humbling the high, and when the King reneged on the special privilege of the Jew - which according to what we learn here, would possibly divest the king of the ability to humble the high and raise the low - shortly afterwards the King had his downfall, and he was not even successful therefore in humbling the Jew].

6. Someone who does not say one thing in his speech and another [lit. one thing] in his heart does not [need to] fear from drowning.

7. The truth brings contentment and abundance.

8. Diarrhea and constipation come as a result of falsehood.

9. Through truth comes the Redemption.

Land of Israel

Part I
1. Through settling the Land of Israel, one perceives Divine Providence over the world.

2. According to the novelties a man derives from the Torah, he draws an illumination from the holiness of the Land of

Israel.

3. According to the longing one has to come to the Land of Israel, through this there is bountiful large income.

4. One who supports many people, through this he draws blessing from Israel to the rest of the world.

5. One who longs for the Land of Israel arouses longing in his mother and father - meaning, in their souls - so they come to Israel, and the Holy One, Blessed be He comes with them, and they wait and long for him [to come to the Holy Land].

6. Through the money one gives to the poor people that live in the Land of Israel, through this his wealth is maintained.

7. One who knows about the Land of Israel, who has truly tasted the taste of the Land of Israel, can recognize in another if he had been by a true tzaddik on Rosh HaShanaor not. For one whom merited being by a true tzaddik on Rosh HaShana, wherever he looks, the air of that place gains the aspect of the air of Israel. Therefore, anyone who knows the taste of the Land of Israel, each person according to his level, will without question sense the Land of Israel when he chances upon and meets with a man who had been by a true tzaddik on Rosh HaShana. For through such a man the air becomes the aspect of the air of the Land of Israel, as explained above.

Clothes

Part I
1. A person's clothes hint at his character traits.

2. One who goes barefoot, it is certain that he sins.

3. As a result of brazenness, one is punished through his clothes, also due to [false] oaths.

4. One who is not careful not to look at his father's nakedness, in the end his children will go naked and barefoot.

5. One who eats before the prayer is punished through his clothes.

6. Due to arrogance, one is punished through his clothes.

7. One who seduces his friend away from the right path to the wrong one, will consequently not have with what to clothe himself.

8. One who is a guarantor for a non-Jews is punished through his clothing.

9. In the future, the Holy One Blessed be He will be avenged from those who dressed in the clothing of non-Jews.

10. One who goes in torn clothing due to poverty, his rectification is through weeping before the Blessed Lord.

11. All who treat clothes with disrespect will end up not benefiting from them.

12. One who makes a garment for a poor person will be saved from humiliations.

13. One who is wary not to embarrass any man merits garments.

Part II
1. Through & telling stories of Tzaddikim, the light of Mashiach is drawn into the world, much darkness and troubles are dispelled from the world, and one also merit having attractive clothing.

Sefer HaMidot

2. One who is accustomed to cursing, through this he will not have clothes for Shabbat.

3. One who always beautifies his legs with fine garments, for example, wearing ostentatious shoes or pants, through this he comes to deceive others.

4. One who is negligent disrespectful in the commandment of tzitzit does not merit burial.

5. One who makes clothing for his friend can change his friend's will in any way he wants, both materially and spiritually.

6. When a man dresses in his father's clothes, through this it is easy for him to practice his father's traits

7. "Come eat my food and drink…" - the initials of the Hebrew words in this verse spell **Lulav** palm branch. "…from the wine…" adding four for the letters of the word has the same gematria numerical value as the initials of Etrog, Hadas, Arava citron, myrtle, willow. The word "Masachti - I mixed…" - is an aspect of Sukkot [in that the words share the same root letters]. [Thus, we derive that] through the mitzvah of taking the Four Species and through [dwelling in] the Sukkah, a man merits to have food, drink and clothing, and also that his soul will receive life-force. Through the sukkah one merits to have clothing, an aspect of "When I put clouds as his garment." Through the willow one merits beverage, through the myrtle one merits to vitalize the soul, and through the lulav and the etrog one merits eating, for they have fruits, which are types of food.

Shame

1. One who humiliates his friend becomes mute and forgets [In the location cited the person forgot his learning].

Sefer HaMidot

2. It is permitted to embarrass the rabbis who lease the rabbinate for the sake of conceit, and it is appropriate to disgrace them, and to make light of their honor, and one should not stand for them, and they should not be called "Rabbi," and the prayer shawl on them is like a mule's saddle.

3. It is better to annul one's Torah study than to humiliate a Jew.

4. One who humiliates a Torah scholar, or one's friend in front of a Torah scholar, is an "apikohrus" [apostate]. He is also called one who is brazen faced against the Torah.

5. The garment of a righteous man atones for the spilling of blood.

6. When people insult you, fast and weep.

7. When shame comes to you, it is only that you should repent for the sins that you commit carelessly [lit. tread on with your heel].

8. Also, shame comes when you rejoice in the pain of your friend.

9. Envision the letters of "Belief" [in Hebrew, Emunah, spelled אמונה] and through this there will not come upon you any shame.

10. Someone who needs to give over a collateral to procure a loan, it is certain that these items which were pledged were contemptible in his eyes in another life.

11. When some shame comes upon a person, he should expect a salvation.

12. One who wants to be shamed [Or feel ashamed] should envision the image of his mother.

Sefer HaMidot

13. Through giving charity for the sake of Heaven, you will come to the trait of abashment.

14. When shame comes upon a person, it is certain that he does not have the quality of trust in GOD.

15. One who digs a pit, in the end he will be shamed [to whatever degree], and sometimes the matter causes him to become the subject of gossip among people.

16. Through having trust in GOD, shame will not come upon him.

17. One who steals from the poor, shame comes upon him.

18. When a person puts you down and embarrasses you, and he is not your enemy; carry and bear the shame, for it is certainly from Heaven that he should berate you. And by this shame, you will be hidden and concealed from the satan, who hates you and is always overbearing upon you and accusing you. Through this shame that you bear from one who is not your enemy, through this the enemy, the satan, will not overbearing on you.

19. Through adulation, you will become an object of derision amongst the [gentile] nations, and the [gentile] nations will curse you and be enraged at you.

20. When someone humiliates you or laughs at you, it is certain that you humiliated his forefathers.

21. When everyone is humiliating you and causing you pain, be silent and do not leave your house [lit. from the entrance of your house].

22. When you are being humiliated, give charity.

23. Through charity, you will merit to the quality of

abashment.

24. Humiliation of a king: The Holy One Blessed be He punishes even a nation that humiliates a different king of a foreign nation.

25. A sinner will be humiliated in the World to Come before his teachers is rabbis. alternate text: forefathers.

26. One who humiliates a Torah scholar will have no healing for his wounds.

27. It is proper that when hearing from a friend a falsehood not to jump and embarrass him, rather hint to him with a motion, so that his friend will recognize that it is not so.

28. It is a mitzva to publicize evildoers.

29. One who is abashed will not readily sin.

30. One who does not have the quality of abashment, it is certain that his forefathers did not stand on Mount Sinai.

31. It is better [lit. easier or more comfortable] for a man to throw himself into a fiery furnace so as not to humiliate his fellowman in public.

32. When your friend humiliates you, agree with his words.

33. One who embarrasses [lit. whitens - because when a person is embarrassed the blood rushes out of his face] his fellowman in public, it is as if he spilled blood, and he descends to Hell and will not rise

34. It is better [lit. easier or more comfortable] for a man to have relations with a woman who might be married than to humiliate his fellowman.

Sefer HaMidot

35. Do not embarrass one of the nations who is committed as you are to the Torah and Commandments. However, it is permitted to humiliate a sinner, and to verbally abuse him.

36. All the gates of prayer are closed, save the gate of one verbally abused.
All things are punished by a messenger, except for verbal abuse, and the Curtain is not locked before it [that is they are very much in the so to speak Divine line of sight until GOD carries out retribution].

Trust

Part I
1. One who has trust in GOD does not have any fear.

2. Through trust in GOD comes peace.

3. Trust in GOD comes through fear of Heaven.

4. Through faith, one will come to trust in GOD.

5. One who doesn't have trust in GOD, he tells lies.

6. Through lies, one cannot have real trust in GOD.

7. One who is confident in the blessed GOD, the Holy One Blessed be He saves him from all troubles, and especially from being murdered.

8. Through trust in GOD, a person does not need to come onto his friend. Also, no person will or can embarrass him.

9. Through trust in GOD, a person is saved from worry.

10. Through trust in GOD, one merits to know holy names.

11. One who does not possess the trait of trust in

Sefer HaMidot

GOD, should guard himself not to embarrass any man, also he should be careful to pray with intention of the heart.

12. One who has trust in GOD will not die before his time.

13. One who does not have trust in GOD should rise before the dawn and say supplications aloud.

14. Through being silent, one will merit to trust in GOD.

15. Through being careful not to shake hands [to seal an agreement - the probable meaning here - as found in a parallel source cited - is that one should be careful not to make agreements with bad people or for bad purposes], one merits to the attribute of trust in GOD. Also, through not associating with the wicked.

16. Through adulation, trust in GOD is lost.

17. The waters of the Jordan are a segulah [propitious] for trust in GOD.

18. Through trust in GOD, a person comes close to the blessed GOD.

19. One who trusts in gentiles, what is his - is will be theirs.

Part II
1. When a person carries out an act with faith, and is ensnared by some type of hitch or violation of the Torah, he should trust that the Holy One, Blessed be He will save him, and the Holy One Blessed He set this pitfall for him, so that he would blaze a path for his descendents in this trapping, that they will be saved from it.

2. One who guards himself from thoughts of idolatry, merits every time to attain trust in GOD, until he [attains such trust that he] does not worry what he will eat tomorrow [even

Sefer HaMidot

though he has nothing for the next day, he trusts the GOD will provide]. This is the level of "Blessed is the Lord, day by day". Through this, the Holy One, Blessed be He does not see wrongdoing or evil in him, and all who harm [lit. touch] him, it is as if they harm [lit. touch] the pupil of GOD's eye so to speak.

House

Part I

1. A house that is uninhabited - beware of entering it, for it is a place of demons.

2. One who has negative experiences in one place should go to another.

3. When a house is fit to be blessed, then when the Tzaddik comes to the house, the blessing comes as well.

4. There are places that are conducive to good fortune, and the opposite is true as well.

5. Relating to the issue of the good and bad that comes to a person in a fashion proximate to natural events, it is all according to the time and place.

6. One who takes revenge out of jealousy destroys his house.

7. The place from where a man exited, he does not have desire for that place - to get from it pleasure.

8. If there is an uneducated hassid one who is overly pious, do not dwell in his neighborhood.

9. Any house in which words of Torah are heard will not be destroyed.

10. A city whose topography has major ascents & descents -

its inhabitants grow old halfway through their lives.

11. If wine is poured out like water in a house, there is blessing.

12. Do not enter a house with idols in it.

13. Someone who wants to enter a house to live in it, he should recite the Torah in its entirety the Five Books of Moses, and it can be divided between many people, and afterwards he can enter to live in it.

14. Someone without land is not a man.

15. There are places which cause one to commit transgressions.

16. Anger and adultery of a woman destroy the house.

17. When the threshold of a house, or its entrances are destroyed, it is an evil omen for the house.

Part II

1. Living on the upper floor of a house is more conducive to serving GOD than living in the bottom floor.

2. Sometimes the construction of the house prevents a woman from conceiving, as when the beams are not placed according to their order from the Six Days of Creation. In such a case, the house is as if it were destroyed, even though it is standing. This destruction comes and harms the woman, and she does not conceive.

3. At the entrance to a man's house, it is discernible if his ancestral merit has finished, or if his ancestral merit is effective.

One needs to be careful, in the building of a house, that it

Sefer HaMidot

should not have in its construction wood from trees that produce fruit.

5. The lumber that is in a structure, if a man merits, it will be in the aspect of "fiery angels standing", and the structure will stand for a long time. If he does not merit - the fiery angels are burned, and thus the fires that abound.

6. When a man builds a wall, and its capstone falls, he should know that this is an evil omen for his progeny.

7. A man does not find satisfaction [lit. enjoy or benefit] unless he dwells in a place where his forefathers dwelled.

8. It is a segulah [auspicious], when one moves into a new house to live, to bring in a sword, knife, or other weapon. A sign for this: "With wisdom the house will be built. "Wisdom" is the acronym for the passage, "Extorted trade are their weapons." "The word "their trade" from this passage shares two definitions, "their swords" and "their dwellings" [as both variations are explained in Rashi there]

9. The cap of a house is a sign for the group or family, concerning what will happen to them.

Crying

1. Someone who cannot cry should look at the sky, for it caused the water to cry.

2. Crying annuls promiscuous thoughts.

3. A segulah for healing sicknesses of the neck is to cry over the destruction of the Temple.

Children
Part I
1. Anyone who cries and mourns over an upright man merits

Sefer HaMidot

to raise his children.

2. One must guard a baby that it should not go [about] with an uncovered head.

3. A man does not need to worry about the income of his children. For as they grow, their income grows with them.

4. One who causes his friend to abstain, even temporarily from the commandment of be fruitful and multiply [that is to engage in kosher relations with his wife, to bring children into the world], will go to Sheol childless.

5. One who forces his wife to have relations with him, even when it is a mitzva, will have children that are not proper upstanding.

6. A woman who bleeds [menstrual blood] excessively, her pain in bringing children into the world is greater [this could also include and insinuate that her raising children is more straining].

7. A daughter of a Cohen [Priestly class] who marries an Israel [common class], and a daughter of a Torah scholar who marries one without education [lit. a person of the land], will not have children [lit. seed].

8. Fasting on Thursdays is auspicious [segula] against the pain of having children [this includes having a safe pregnancy, childbirth, and raising the infant].

9. The modesty of a woman merits her to have upstanding children.

10. Through the joy of the festivals, and through the proper donning of tefillin, one's wife will give birth to sons.

11. Sometimes, when one does not have children, and others

Sefer HaMidot

pray for him that he should have children, he dies.

12. For the sin of, not upholding one's, vows children die.

13. Change of habitat causes, the ability to have children.

14. Grown children do not die for the sins of their fathers. But in a place where the Name of GOD is profaned, even grown children die.

15. One who eats meat and drinks wine will have healthy children.

16. One who looks at the heel of a woman, or at his wife when she

17. One who lives ten years in the land of Israel and does not have children should divorce his wife, lest he did not merit to [have his lineage] built by her.

18. What should a man do to have male children? He should marry a woman who is fitting to him, sanctify himself at the time of marital relations, and ask for sons, from the One to whom all sons belong.

19. Anyone who begets a child, brings forth a child similar to himself.

20. A man should beware not to cut down a tree before its time, for this harm the raising of his children.

21. All who pursue [giving] charity, merit to have sons who are wealthy, wise, and proficient in the homiletic section of the Torah.

22. What should a man do to have children? He should spread his wealth to the poor, and cheer his wife before relations with her.

Sefer HaMidot

23. Just as it is forbidden to murder a man, so it is forbidden to cut down a fruit tree before its time.

24. Yoav, who did not leave a son similar to him [in his stead], it is said of him that he died. David, who did leave a son similar to him in his stead, it is said of him that he layed to rest.

25. One who has a daughter first, the evil eye will not have power over him.

26. One who raises an orphan in his home is as if he gave birth to him.

27. One who teaches his friend's son Torah is as if he gave birth to him.

28. Forty days [of the beginning of a pregnancy, which is] before the creation of the fetus, one should pray that his wife will give birth to a son.

29. One who thinks about promiscuity, his wife also comes to have such thoughts. And when his wife has promiscuous thoughts, the husks [evil forces] come to her [have relations with her] in a dream, and through this her children die.

30. One who is promiscuous causes that his wife will commit adultery on him.

31. One who burns his friend's crops will not leave a son to inherit him.

32. A woman who miscarriages - at the time of birth, place an apple on her head.

33. One who does a mitzvah [commandment or good deed] and does not finish it, buries his wife and children.

Sefer HaMidot

34. One who marries a woman for the sake of money will have improper children, and will lose the money in a short time.

35. One who is involved in learning Torah and acts of kindness will merit to have many children.

36. Children do not die for the sins of their fathers, unless they grasp the deeds of their father's in their hands, that is continue in their path of sin.

37. Marital relations during pregnancy are beneficial to the fetus to beautify it [literally: lighten it], make it more agile, and possessor of fine form and strength.

38. One who does not have children should accept upon himself to go into exile.

39. One who goes down into his fellow's business, that is begins to compete with him is as if he committed adultery with his friend's wife.

40. When a man is delivered into the hands of his enemies, it is as if he lost his children.

41. Someone who had sexual relations with a Kutaite woman [this was a large group that converted to Judaism, but in reality, kept serving idolatry] or a male, or had idolatrous contemplations, will not have a son who is a Torah scholar, and if his son does learn Torah, he will be forgetful.

42. Good children are a great healing to their fathers.

43. Through falsehood, the children die.

44. One who does not separate from his wife in anticipation of her days of impurity, even if he should have children like those of Aharon, they will die. In contrast, one who does separate from his wife at that time, he will have sons who are fitting to be legal deciders.

45. One who does havdalah on wine at the closing of the Shabbat will have male children who are fitting to be legal deciders.

46. One who sanctifies himself in marital relations through conducting himself modestly will have sons.

47. One should be very careful that one's child is not nursed by an evil woman. For milk contaminates and milk purifies.

48. Bathing in hot water, and anointing one's self with oil give health to the fetus.

49. One who does not hold himself back from urinating, his prayers on behalf of his children will be heard.

50. The fetus develops according to the form of the father and mother.

51. Bad mannerism in a person's house is worse than the War of Gog and Magog [a war of immense proportions that, according to prophecy, will take place right before the Redemption].

52. One should come to synagogue early and stay late, and his children will have longevity [lit. his children's days will be lengthened].

53. One should not treat one son differently than his other sons.

54. Through Channukah and the candles of Shabbat, one will have sons who will be Torah scholars.

55. Whoever loves the sages will be given sons who become sages. Whoever honors sages are given sages as sons-in-law.

56. Through the sins of [not fulfilling] oaths, also for the sin desisting from Torah study, also for the sin of [faulty or lacking of] mezuzot, also for the sin of [faulty or lacking of] tzitzit, also for the sin of causeless hatred, children die when they are young.

57. One who gives ma'aser [tithe] of his money, his children are saved from the sickness of Samkah ["red"]

58. Small children [lit. infants of the house of their rabbi], retribution is exacted upon them, for the [sins of the] generation.

59. Through smelling myrtle on Shabbat, one merits having children who will be Torah scholars.

60. A woman who miscarries her children, segulah [spiritual benefit/protection] for this, is for her to bathe a bride the wedding ceremony.

61. According to how a man eats, so will be his sons and daughters.

62. One whose sons die should not have marital relations during the week, only from Shabbat to Shabbat.

63. The drawing of a bow on Lag b'Omeris a segulah [spiritual benefit] for children. Also, praying before the pulpit with melody is a segulah for children.

64. One must teach a child proper behavior ["derech eretz"] from a young age.

65. The songs and praises that are said before dawn are a segulah for children. It is also helpful for a woman deficient in her milk, and for an evil woman who is bad-tempered.

Sefer HaMidot

66. One who belittles himself before his rabbi by asking about all his doubts, even though his rabbi embarrasses him [for it] - through this, he will merit to have a child who is greater in Torah than his rabbi.

67. One who accepts suffering with love will merit to have children who will live long.

68. The acts of GOD [lit. Hashem - the Name] follow after the name of a man, for a name has causative [power].

69. One who raises his voice in order to glorify himself, his children will be brought into captivity.

70. One who doesn't have children should use oil regularly.

71. And sometimes one should uproot his dwelling, and his children will live.

72. Through pursuing peace, one saves his children from death and exile.

73. Someone who does something, and afterwards it becomes a stumbling block for others, good is denied to his children.

74. Sometimes, because of the great love between a man and his wife, she does not conceive.

75. Usually, when barren women conceive, they give birth to a son.

76. Through verbal abuse, children die.

77. A tzaddik possesses the power to curse a man, that his children will not be proper.

78. One who has the Tzaddik as a guest by him, is

blessed with children.

79. One who longs to do a mitzvah [commandment or good deed], but does not merit to do it, through this longing he will merit having children who inherit his greatness, and eventually will do that mitzvah.

80. One who deprives someone's livelihood, his children will eventually die.

81. A magnet is a segulah [spiritual benefit] for children.

82. One's children die as a result of working with impure names, or sorcery, or believing in them.

83. When a man and his wife wash their hands and give charity before relations, through this they remove the spirit of impurity from the children they conceive.

84. There is woman who raise only girls and not boys.

85. Saying the scriptural passages about tzitzit with self sacrifice, and with great awe, and also clothing the naked, though this one merits one to have male children.

86. A year in which there is blessing in the produce, this is an indication that the Jews will be fruitful and have many children.

87. A woman who deals in witchcraft, her children die and she becomes a widow.

88. A nursing woman whose milk is deficient, the segula auspicious act for this is for her husband to mourn over Jerusalem.

89. Violence [lit. beatings] comes upon one's sons through falsehood. Location can also be a cause.

Sefer HaMidot

90. One who gives joy to a bride and groom will merit that his wife will birth sons.

91. Also, through being careful with candles, one merits sons.

92. A year with abundant rain is a sign that in that year, many sons will be born.

93. A man and his wife who curse each other will not raise their children.

94. A segulah for raising children: Plant any type of crop, and when you harvest it, give it to the poor - do not benefit from it yourself.

95. One who casts excessive fear upon his generation, will not uphold wise [literally: wise of heart] children.

96. One who does not have mercy on his children, it is certain known that he does not possess a portion of the holy intelligence.

97. When he does not review his learning [and forgets it], through this the children die.

98. Through sexual immorality, one will not raise children.

99. The name Elo-kah, one of names of GOD, gives protection to children.

100. One who strives to assure an income to people who seek GOD, will merit that his children not go off [develop, turn out] into bad ways.

101. Through faith in the tzaddik, one's children live and prosper.

102. When a male child comes into the world, kindness

comes to the world.

103. One who causes his father and mother pain will not merit to raise sons.

104. One who pursues peace, through this he will merit seeing his childrens' children.

105. Breakage to a door or a window is a sign of weakness in one's children.

106. Contention is a bad sign for [having] children and peace is a good sign.

107. Children will be fools when their father is bad tempered.

108. Through respecting [your] father, you will merit having male children.

Part II

1. One who suffers in the raising of his children [this includes having children], should read the Biblical passages describing the Creation, everyday. Also, throug this reading, one is saved from the accusations of being a thief.

2. A segulah for having children is humbling oneself.

3. Planting a vineyard is damaging to the growth of fetuses.

4. Endeavoring to free captives is a segulah for giving birth.

5. The saying of the ma'amadotis helpful for having children.

6. A woman whose children die from the disease called samkah- that is, zedushin- should wash them in oil, and then burn this oil afterwards while performing a ritual immersion.

Sefer HaMidot

7. One against whom many arise to challenge him on account of his faith; and he stands up against them and makes well-received counter-claims, through this he will merit having many children, and the world will be filled with his seed.

8. The letter hey [fifth letter of the Hebrew alphabet] made out of silver, is a segulah for propagation.

9. Sometimes the construction of the house prevents a woman from birthing, as when the beams are not placed according to their order from the Six Days of Creation. In such a case, the house is as if it were destroyed, even though it is standing. This destruction comes and harms the woman, and she does not give birth.

10. One must look for a mohel who is righteous and GOD fearing. For when the mohel is not fitting, it can happen that the child, when he is grown, will not be able to have children [lit. cause birth]. Also, when the mohel is not fitting, the child can, GOD forbid, come to suffer from "falling disease" often translated as epilepsy.

11. A deceased person who has a son involved in studying the Torah, is as if he never died.

12. The milk of a righteous woman is good for a child's [lit. baby's] fear of Heaven, and also gives him dominion over this world.

13. Death of one's children, GOD forbid, comes through causing one's friend to fall away from his faith.

14. When there is peace in a country's government, the Jews give birth to master teachers.

15. One who guards himself in, as well as the season and time of, sexual relations, that they are balanced - that is to say, that neither he nor the season is too hot or too cold –

Sefer HaMidot

through this, the children born to him will be great sages.

16. One who has control over his desires causes that his children will not be drawn to evil ways, that his money is blessed, and that he will not be put to a test.

17. Even a woman who is righteous, but not of respected lineage, will have unworthy children.

18. In a time of abundant grain in the world, it is a sign that males will be born. In a time of abundant wine, it is a sign for the birth of females.

19. One who does not have a son should accustom himself to bring gifts to Torah scholars, and say the section of Torah verses about the first-fruit offering. Also, he should increase his study of Talmud, and minimize his study of Aggadah, for studying Aggadah is a segulah for having girls.

20. By learning the codes of Jewish law until one is able to render halachicdecisions, one causes a number of barren women to conceive.

21. Sometimes, through being held in prison, one is saved from being barren of children.

22. Through charity one merits to have children.

23. A segulahfor a woman who is having difficulty giving birth is to hang the keys to the cemetery from her neck. This is also a segulah for becoming pregnant.

24. Children die, GOD forbid, by seeing a seminal emission.

25. There are trees which, when their wood is used to make one's bed, hinder birth and raising children. Conversely, there are trees which promote birth and raising children.

Sefer HaMidot

26. One who has had children die at a young age should have his living child's mother makes a coat that he should wear always, until he matures.

27. When the Jews are fruitful and multiply, the non-Jewish nations make new harsh decrees upon us.

28. Self-mortification is helpful for giving birth.

29. Thorns are fortuitous for giving birth.

30. Someone who is born circumcised, it is certain that his imagination is good and pleasant.

Blessing

1. The one who is blessed should give the one who blessed him a gift.

2. The blessing of a non-Jew should not be insignificant in your eyes.

3. One who brings those who are far, close to the service of the Blessed Lord, the blessings are given over to his hands. is empowered to grant blessings.

Tiding

Part I
1. One who is accustomed to saying good tidings, he is enclothed with an aspect of Eliyahu [Elijah].

2. Do not bear bad tidings, for due to bad tidings numerous people have passed away.

3. One who fulfills a commandment 'as it was said' There are different interpretations as to what this demand. The Maharsha explains that it means - for the sake of Heaven. The

Sefer HaMidot

Maharal explains it means - in completion, exactly as it was commanded, evil tidings do not come to him, and the Holy One, Blessed be He, decrees, and he annuls.

4. One who bears evil tidings falls into small-mindedness.

Part II
1. One who is accustomed to bear good tidings, through this his feet will not hurt him.

Arrogance

1. The Messiah will not come until all the arrogance in the world ceases.

2. Through arrogance, one comes to homosexual desires, also one comes to anger. Also, sometimes a woman cannot conceive because she overly adorns herself and is arrogant.

3. Through arrogance, famine comes to the world.

4. Through arrogance, one comes to drunkenness and vice-versa.

5. Through arrogance, one comes to be frightened.

6. A segula [auspicious] to annul arrogance, is to give charity.

7. One who arrogantly imposes rabbinical authority, God arouses enemies against him.

8. One who experiences an uplifted heart, should know that the hour [time] is successful for him.

9. One who saves poor people has power in his gaze on arrogant people to humble them.

10. One who walks in a public marketplace and falls, for certain he has a large ego.

11. Conducive to overcoming arrogance: to take part in the suffering of the Jews.

12. A poor man who is pursued by a wicked man; know that the poor man is haughty.

13. Pride causes a loss of faith.

14. Pride blocks one's heart and eyes from perceiving the Blessed God's wonders and from experiencing awe before Him.

15. One should not find cause to be haughty due to brilliant perceptions or good deeds, for it all comes by way of the tzadik of the generation and one is merely by the tzadik like a pen by a scribe.

16. Eating and drinking bring to arrogance.

17. A rectification for arrogance is that one should fast.

18. Conducive to [overcoming] arrogance; to look at the sky.

19. A person is spooked by nightmares in order to A person is spooked by nightmares in order to remove embedded arrogance, which is concealed from him, which he doesn't discern.

20. Anyone who is conceited; his wisdom and prophecy [possibly: intuition] depart.

21. An arrogant pauper is unbearable to the intellect. He, too, eventually has regret and is despised in his own eyes.

22. An egotist [someone beautiful] is unable to humble his self-regard and will come to forgetfulness.

23. A conceited person is, considered physically, handicapped.

24. Depending upon the necessity of the matter, it may be permissible to act in a way which appears arrogant.

25. An arrogant person will eventually commit adultery. He is like an idolater, like one who denies the essentials of faith, like one who committed all forms of incest, and like one who built an alter for idolatry. His importance diminishes to nothing, he deserves to be chopped down like the idolatrous Asherah tree. His remains will not be stirred for the resurrection and the Shekhinah wails over him.

26. Wearing a Tzaddik's hat is conducive to removing arrogance. hence the Nanach beanie.

27. Through faith, you will be able to break yourself from pride, and rule over the vice of arrogance.

28. An arrogant person, his thoughts [plans] are unsuccessful.

29. When you happen upon a transgression without awareness, it is certain that you have arrogance, and through this accidental sin, Heaven is showing you that you are not yet a tzaddik.

30. When any conceit comes to you, be concerned from calamity befalling you.

31. A poor man of humble spirit, even though he doesn't give charity, he is better than a prideful rich man, even though he gives charity.

32. When pride falls upon you, visualize before you your father's image.

33. Arrogance is a sign of or for downfall, God forbid.

34. Arrogance is a result of your not having rectified the sins of youth.

35. One who's wine sours, it is certain that he is haughty.

36. One who is haughty, his dwelling place will not endure.

37. One who has arrogance, I God and he cannot dwell together in the world. Even a slight breeze troubles him. His prayer goes unheeded. He does not have healing. He becomes impoverished in Torah, and his wife denigrates him.

38. One who dons the garb of a Torah scholar and he is not a Torah scholar, will not be brought into God's partition.

39. Pride holds back the coming of Messiah, and confounds a person from the world.

40. The verse - "If his height rises to the sky, and his head reaches the clouds, he will be eternally destroyed like dung, those that look upon him will say, where is he". And the verse - "For refuge is not forever, and is the crown of wealth lasting for generations" are conducive to breaking haughtiness.

Theft

Part I

1. One whose heart is tempted to steal openly, since he has permitted himself to steal from his fellow, he is poised to commit any sin, and there is no remedy to turn him away from his evil way.

2. Through the sin of stealing, the locusts arise, and there is famine, and people eat the flesh of their children.

3. Someone who does not benefit others with his money,

Sefer HaMidot

through these robbers come upon him.

4. One who steals the worth of a penny from his fellow, it is as if he takes away his soul, and the soul of his sons and daughters, and even if he stole indirectly.

5. Someone who does not have regard for his friend's money, it is certain that he is a thief.

6. Ona'at mamon [monetary wrong] overreaching, that is the seller overcharging or the buyer underpaying by one-fifth or one-sixth, is permissible if one overreaches a heathen.

7. Someone who clenches his hand shut from giving charity, robbers come upon him.

8. One who puts his trust in gentiles, in the end they take from him by force.

9. Through judges and teachers of children, that aren't good, also butchers, through this the enemies consume the livelihood of the Jewish people.

10. One who dilutes his beverage with water, thieves come upon him. [This refers to a shopkeeper who has the beverage for sale, and is not a directive never to dilute beverages, this can be learned from the placement of this adage under theft, and also from the fact that this is a topic discussed in the Talmud].

11. Someone who takes a portion from a robbery, in the end the matter will be exposed.

12. A city in which there are thieves, it is certain that the Rabbi likes bribery.

13. Through empty words and conversation, thieves come.

Sefer HaMidot

14. It is permissible to deceive others in order to save a Jewish soul.

15. Concerning one who humiliates his friend, in the end he will give false testimony, in order to steal money.

16. One who has trust in GOD from his early years is saved from robbers.

17. Through hearing foolish words, thieves come.

18. Through falsehood, thieves come.

Part II
1. Through deception, comes - GOD forbid - sickness of the lungs and chest.

2. Through deception, come thoughts of promiscuity with a gentile woman.

3. Through theft, one loses cognizance.

4. Theft harms the eyes.

5. Through saying Tikkun Chatzot [midnight rectification] one is saved from thieves.

6. Someone who has pain raising children [This Hebrew term can refer to not having children at all, perhaps due to miscarriages, or to the travails of raising healthy children, safe from illness, death, or misconduct] should read the [passage in the Torah describing the] Story of Creation every day. Also, through this reading he is saved from being accused of stealing.

Judge

1. Any judge who judges truthfully - his judgments will

Sefer HaMidot

not be annulled, and they prevail even against the will of the litigants.

2. As a result of Torah law or resolutions of a Torah court weakening, through this livelihood shrinks, also the opposite is true. The commentators do not provide a citation, so I suggest the opening verse of the Book of Judges [Shoftim].

3. Through the appointment of judges who are unworthy, come idolatrous thoughts.

4. Through marrying a Torah sage, worthy judges are appointed.

5. Through proper judges, the Torah is beloved in the world.

6. Due to the insults which the judges are insulted, the crops - plagues or curse fall upon it.

7. Through the insults which judges of Israel are insulted, through this inflation occurs in the world.

8. When an evil person becomes great, it becomes hard to deduce novel reasoning in Torah law, and also the words of judges are not accepted or coherent by the litigants.

9. The renewal of national and local taxes is through the judges. This is regarding a spiritual relation between the two, rather than a simplistic description of the work of the judge.

Cognizance

Part I
1. Sometimes GOD brings things upon a person, so that through them the person will understand His mercy and GODliness.

2. Someone whose mind is confused should frequently say

Sefer HaMidot

the prayer of Habakuk

3. Also [for a confused mind], it is a segulah to learn "Sifte Cohen" [Cohen's Lips - commentary on the Shulchan Aruch - Code of Jewish Law], also eating wheat.

4. People's food conceive character in a person according to their, the foods' character.

5. The taste of wheat brings cognizance [da'as] to man.

6. Wine and fragrance tune up one's cognizance.

7. Dissension causes the mind to be unsettled.

8. A person suffers more from what he sees with his eyes than the pain that he feels from information.

9. One who engages in the study of Torah and doing of kindness merits understanding.

10. Through eating bread in the morning [pas shacharis], one becomes wise.

11. The Holy One, Blessed be He, emanates temporary prophecy to a prophet sent on a mission, even if he is not a sage.

12. The sages can grasp with wisdom many concepts that natural intelligence cannot conceive.

13. One who wants to become wise should turn south, when praying - Rash"i.

14. When a person wants to know what to do in a given situation, he should open up a holy book, and he will understand what to do.

Sefer HaMidot

15. Olive oil tunes up the cognizance of the heart.

16. One who goes in simplicity becomes intelligent.

17. One who has faith, merits afterward to serve GOD with great cognizance.

18. Through awe, one merits to cognizance.

19. Through being acquainted with righteous people, one merits to understanding and cognizance.

20. One who conducts himself with modesty has mental clarity.

21. What is seen with the eye, that thing is easier to understand.

22. One who guards himself from food cooked by a non-Jew and wine impurified by a non-Jew, merits wisdom, and understands every book he studies.

23. One who is arrogant does not merit to understand GOD's dominion over everything.

24. When you don't do kindness, through this you don't have cognizance.

25. If you do any damage, you should know that you violated your cognizance.

26. When a certain understanding is revealed to a person, it is certain that he will soon be raised some height.

26. When one repents with all his heart, GOD grants his heart to know His desire and will.

27. One who has not rectified his sins, cannot have a

relationship with GOD, and know GOD.

28. Through truth, you merit to know the ways of GOD.

29. Also, through hosting guests.

30. When you do kindness of truth or truthful kindness to the righteous, you merit to know that all the ways - of prayer, of eating, and of all the other pleasures - are all the Way of GOD.

31. Through joyous singing, one will be a cognizant person.

32. One who is repaid with evil for the good he did, the Holy One, Blessed is He, has mercy on him and grants him great intelligence in the service of the Creator.

33. According to the measure with which a man increases doing good deeds, so the Holy One, blessed is He, deepens his intelligence, that is, He gives him a great mind.

Part II

1. Know, that every world and every creation have its own unique structure and unique construction. For example, the lion's profile is different than that of the sheep: in its strength, and in the structure of its limbs, and its voice. Also, within the species of the lion itself, there is a distinction between each one. Further, in all the created beings, their differences are all encoded in the image of the letters and their permutations. One who merits understanding the Torah can understand the code of all the differences between the creations, and will also know their unification - that is, their origins and purposes and beginnings and endings. For in origin and purpose or beginning and end, they are united without differentiation.

2. Know, that according to greatness of one's knowledge of the Torah and of the natural world, so the world is placed and

Sefer HaMidot

committed in his charge. Thus, the lions were subdued under Daniel, for Daniel was a great sage, and no secret was concealed from him, and he knew the nature of the lion. Nature acts according to the wisdom of the Torah, and it is under the power of that wisdom. [Transcriber's note: I heard from our Teacher, Rabbi Natan, may the memory of the tzadik be for blessing, that this paragraph - 2, is connected to the one above it - **1**, to what is explained there, "One who merits understanding the Torah can understand the code of all the differences between the creations etc." because this is the aspect of all the natural phenomena of the world, and building on this comes article **2**, "Know, that according to the greatness of one's knowledge of the Torah and of the natural world," that is according to how much one merits to understand the permutations of the letters of the Torah, because according to the greatness of his understanding of the letters of the Torah and their permutations etc. so too will be the greatness of his knowledge of the nature of the world, understand this. Refer to Likutey Halachot, Yoreh Deah, Laws of Circumcision, Law 5, article 23 and 24, until the end of the chapter. See there a wondrous explanation of this, and it will forever pleasant for you. The truth is, whoever looks with a good eye, with a true eye, with a straight heart, does not have any problems with this. The opposers somehow took this entry and tried to use it for bad ends, on the contrary, from here can be seen the wondrous greatness of GOD and his true tzadikim. [The opposers who speak against the venerated tzadik, who from the start look at his books with a bad eye, seeking and searching to make a libel, no explanation would be sufficient. For after all these words and truth, he will search and seek to accuse and wrong, to speak against the above mentioned tzadik and his students, may their merit protect us, venerated, with haughtiness and scoffing. Even still I was unable to hold back from presenting what I heard a little about this, and the truth endures, whereas lies are ephemeral, and GOD is forever true, and will save us from double edged sword, just like His Mercy, Blessed is He, helped us until now, amen so should be His Will. Also see

Sefer HaMidot

Likutey Moharan, I:19 in the Teaching of "The Prayer of Chabakuk", and you will understand a little, and also see teaching 17].

3. Through the comprehension a person reaches, that the Holy One, Blessed is He, is One, and that there is no other beside Him, through this he forces the angels of heaven to form into a golem and embark to do his bidding.

4. When thoughts of idol worship come to a person, and he nullifies them by thinking of his faith in GOD, then his thoughts become an aspect of dew of blessing. Also, through this, his mind has fortitude and does not ever become confused; even when the mind becomes tired from pondering some deep concept, then the Holy One, Blessed be He, arranges for him thoughts which relax his mind.

5. Through the merit of those who sustain the poor, the masses are saved from plagues. Also, in their merit, expanded consciousness precedes constricted consciousness [This is the secret of the first night of Passover, as discussed at great length in the holy Nanach books, especially Likutay Halachos].

6. Even in wantonness and foolishness there is wisdom.

7. The voice that emanates from a holy intelligent person is a segula [conducive] to awe.

8. Through confusion of the mind, one's sense of awe is damaged. Also, through confusion of the mind, one's dominion falters.

9. The sages of the generation are the clothing of the generation. According to their wisdom, so too will be the drawing close to GOD and the spiritual perception of the generation. Or the opposite - that is, becoming distanced from GOD, Blessed is He, GOD forbid. In the future, there will be no need to attain GODliness through smarts, for there will the fulfillment of the verse "your teachers will no longer enclothe you..." [Yeshiyahu 30:20].

10. One who wants to have deep comprehension and contemplate some issue, needs to attach his intellect to the Holy Temple. A sign for this can be learned from the verses, "I raise my cognizance to the distance", and "and he saw the place meaning the site of the Temple in the distance."

11. Through faith, the mind is settled.

12. Through converts, cognizance is increased in the world.

13. Even the prophets only know what the Holy One, Blessed is He, reveals to them.

14. One who is a man of great physical might does not have much cognizance.

15. Large steps confuse the mind from in-depth study.

16. Through stealing, one loses cognizance.

17. When the coarseness of one comes into the thoughts of his friend, and the coarseness of the friend come into his thoughts, from this is created the ceiling of the world.

Travel

Part I

1. One who wants to cross the sea, should take with him a bird and an ocean fish, and this is propitious [segula] to cross the sea peacefully and safely.

2. One who cheers himself with the joy of a groom and bride as they exit the marriage canopy, will not be hurt on the way

Sefer HaMidot

[his travels].

3. In the hour that the wagon drivers busy themselves with the carriage and with the horses, say the Wayfarer's Prayer.

4. A segula [propitious] for someone who is traveling on the sea, he should take plaster or lime with him, and he will be saved.

5. Someone who arranges parnassa [income or livelihood] for the tzadikim is assured that GOD will protect him, both on the road and on the sea.

6. Someone riding on a horse should take with him Hoshanot [one of the four species taken on Succot].

7. When you want to travel, bind yourself first with the trait of trust in GOD, and through this, you will not stumble [lit. your feet will not be smitten].

8. When you set out on a journey, give to charity first.

9. All the ways that a person traverses, it is all from the blessed GOD and they are the will of GOD. However, there is no one who can understand his way except for someone who is humble.

10. When you carry with you stones that are found across the field, you will be saved from wild animals.

11. The prayer of Yonah the Prophet is propitious to say on the sea.

12. Through accompanying a guest on his way out, the person, the guest is protected from all harm on the way.

13. One who has no one to accompany him on his journey, should engage in learning Torah.

Sefer HaMidot

14. A person acquires the place where he goes.

Part II
1. Through confession, one cause that the Holy One Blessed is He brings teachers of small children that teach faithfully.

2. Also, one causes the roads to be repaired from stumbling blocks.

3. Danger on the roads comes as a result of sexual impurity [lit. violation of the covenant]. A hint for this from the Torah: "my going and resting you have encompassed etc." these Hebrew words can also be translated as my seed you have scattered - thus hinting that by the scattering of one's seed, that is sexual impurity, one's travel will be endangered.

4. Through traveling the ways, a man gains the ability of understanding [the Hebrew word here is "mavin" - very similar to the English usage].

5. On a night that you have a nightmare [lit. fear at the time of sleep], do not travel in the day.

6. Traveling The roads brings a person to evil speech [lushon hura], idolatry, promiscuity, and spilling blood, and these sins diminish one's livelihood.

7. Broad steps confuse the intellect from in depth study.

Instruction

1. Someone who rules legal Jewish law decisions and he is submissive to those greater than him, through this the Holy One Blessed He will guard him that he should not stumble in a matter of a legal decision.

2. A place of hora'ah is conducive to fear of GOD.

3. When food in a person's house becomes non-kosher through the mixing of the forbidden with the permitted, and there is not enough of the permitted to annul the forbidden, this is a sign, he is being shown from Above, that the person has caused a blemish in some supernal unification and conjugation. For the unification and conjugation is the aspect of the forbidden being annulled in the permitted, the aspect of GOD returns individual's home. He frees those imprisoned [asirim] in auspicious times [kosherot]."

4. When there is peace with the government, through this there is born in Israel the Jewish people children who develop into instructors of the halacha.

5. One who is strict with others and lenient with himself, and claims he heard things he did not hear; through this he does not merit to see the beauty of the King. For the klipa [evil force] of Edom, which is bad fear, darkens the light of his eyes so that he cannot gaze upon the beauty of the countenance of the King.

6. Through promiscuity, one falls into captivity, or sickness of pain in his feet. Also, a student who has not reached the level of giving [legal-halacha] instruction and instructs, falls to this. Also, destructive forces dominate him.

Hospitality

Part I

1. One who does not take in guests strengthens the hand of evildoers, that they will not return in repentance.

2. A city that does not practice hospitality comes to sexual immorality, and through that it comes to murder.

3. Hospitality merits a woman to have sons.

Sefer HaMidot

4. Receiving guests is comparable to receiving the Shabbat.

5. One who hosts a Torah scholar in his home, it is considered as if he had offered the daily burnt offerings.

6. Receiving guests is greater than coming early to the house of worship or welcoming the Divine Presence.

7. Those who have no rabbis in their surroundings are comparable to Cutiim [Samaritans].

Part II

1. Through practicing hospitality, fear of GOD rests upon all beings.

2. Receiving guests is a segulah for returning a woman to her fertility cycle.

3. Through sanctifying GOD's name, the leadership of the heads of the generation gains power and might. Through this, the commandment of hospitality gains importance in the eyes of all, and through this the scholar's merit that the law is decided according to their opinion.

Sweetening of Judgements

Part I

1. At the time when suffering is sent upon a person, it is sworn not commence [lit. go or embark] except on a specific day, and not to desist [lit. leave] except on a specific day and a specific hour, and through a specific medication. However, repentance, prayer and charity annul the oath.

2. Being disheartened [lit. weakness of the mind], that is to say, depression, draws bad fortune upon one, and when one's fortune is bad, the aspect of harsh judgment dominates.

3. The scriptural verses about the Choshen [breast plate worn by the high priest] is a tikun [rectification or remedy] for dinim.

4. When a person has pain, he should give charity. For the charity is like he's paying for the judgment, and through this the dinim [defined at the beginning of this entry] are lightened [lit. sweetened]. Because someone who takes payment to judge, his rulings are void.

5. What is the extent of suffering.

6. Anyone who has gone forty days without suffering, he has received his world [that is he cashed in all the pleasantness that was destined for him], and disasters are prepared for him.

7. One who chastises his fellow for the sake of Heaven, a thread of kindness is extended upon him.

8. Three things call attention to one's sins: A leaning wall when one passes under it, prayer with concentration. when this is brought on by one's reliance and anticipation to see the prayers answered, and one who brings prosecution on his friend [when one asks Heaven to bring retribution on someone, this arouses question of his own good standing].

9. Four things tear up the bad edict on a man: Charity, crying out, changing one's name, and changing one's deeds.

10. Crying out helps an individual specifically before the edict.

11. A Heavenly decree that is accompanied by an oath, even for a group, cannot be torn.

12. Through fasting in years of famine, one is saved from a strange death.

Sefer HaMidot

13. When some decree is decreed on a person, it is decreed on him specifically for a certain place. Through this he can save himself with a change of place.

14. One who has pain in his eyes or stomach pains, it is certain that dinim see title of this entry rest upon him.

15. One should make his suffering known to the public, and the public will ask in prayer for mercy on his behalf.

16. When there is some din judgement or contention on the Jewish People, GOD forbid, the Holy One Blessed He notifies the tzadikim, so that they should pray for Israel, and whomever does not pray for them, the Holy One Blessed He is angry with them.

17. When a man sees that dinim are weighing on him, he should talk about his enemies and justify them.

18. Through the appointing of kosher judges, hardships are annulled.

19. One who made a vow and did not fulfill his vow, the Holy One Blessed He brings suffering upon him. When he is silent [in response], it is considered as if he has fulfilled his vow, some understand this to mean that it is as if he fulfilled the original vow, for this is the progression of this adage. However, if this were the case the text should have been 'his vow' - which in Hebrew is a simple one letter suffix, the actual text is, 'a vow'.

20. One who accepts suffering with love, it is considered as if he offered a sacrifice.

21. When a man is walking and falls, it is a sign that he was met out from Above for a failure.

Through immersing in a mikveh, suffering is annulled and salvation comes.

23. When some harsh decree is passed on a man, before people know about it, it is easily overturned.

24. One who becomes weak in [lit. falls from] his faith should know that he is being judged from Above.

25. One who has dinim upon him should look frequently [lit. every time] upon the heavens.

26. One who shows the good path to evildoers, the Holy One Blessed He justifies him in judgment.

27. Through Truth, the Holy One Blessed He does with him kindness that is not dressed in din.

28. That which the Holy One Blessed He hides His Countenance from you, it is because of the blasphemy that is within you.

29. Through trust in GOD, the judgment is sweetened and kindness is drawn forth.

30. Through faith, you can direct the blessed GOD to do your will.

31. Through charity, one transforms judgment and din to the attribute of kindness.

32. Someone who does not have faith, it is certain that the Holy One Blessed He has removed His kindness from him.

33. When harsh decrees prevail, and kindness is rare [lit. precious] and not found, know that crying is helpful for this. [I heard from his holy mouth, at the time when I transcribed this before him, that a hint for this is in the verse: "How precious is Your kindness, GOD" - Explaining as follows,

Sefer HaMidot

when kindness is rare precious, and unavailable, that is dinim prevail GOD forbid, then the action to be taken for this: the continuation of the verse - "And people in the shadow of Your wings take refuge." The initials [of the last three words] spell out "crying", because crying helps for this, as previously stated].

34. Through cognizance, kindness is drawn forth.

35. Through giving charity to an upright man, you will merit to draw kindness also to your friends.

36. Someone who does not accept rebuke, suffering comes upon him.

37. To sweeten dinim, recite Tehillim Psalms, Chapter 39.

38. Someone who strengthens himself before prayer and prepares himself thoroughly [lit. large], even if afterwards he does not pray appropriately, through this suffering separates from him.

39. To sweeten dinim, say learn Mishnayot of Zeraim [The first of the six sections of the mishna].

40. Sometimes the Holy One Blessed He expends all the suffering on the father, so that his son will have peace.

41. Through making a vow, the fury of the blessed GOD is forestalled.

42. To sweeten dinim, say Tehillim, Psalms Chapter 77.

43. Someone who attaches himself at night to the quality of faith, the din upon him is sweetened.

44. Through arrogance, kindness departs rising above to the heaven.

Sefer HaMidot

45. Through saying Tikkun Chatzot [Midnight Rectification - special regiment of prayers said at midnight], the judgment is sweetened.

46. When you stay awake the whole night, by this you are saved from dinim.

47. By the troubles that are not upon man, he can attain and understand his iniquities.

48. Through that which one comes to the Tzaddik, the coming in its own right can sweeten the dinim.

49. Also, the money that is given to the Tzaddik, the giving itself sweetens the din.

50. Due to depression, thoughts are aligned in Heaven for his detriment.

51. Through learning the Torah, accusers will retreat.

52. When one who goes and falls occasionally, he had been decreed to die, and now it is annulled through the falling

53. For the evil decrees that the nations decree on Israel, they should say Tehillim, Psalms Chapter 62.

54. Through staying in a mikva under the water, until one can no longer hold his breath, the din is sweetened.

55. Sometimes wine arouses din.

56. One who gives his bread to someone lacking cognizance, suffering comes upon him.

57. Someone without cognizance eventually is exiled.

58. A judgment that was forestalled overnight, the judgment is annulled.

59. One who learns Torah for the sake of Heaven, sets peace in the Upper Tribunal and in the Lower Tribunal.

60. One who reads a scriptural verse in its time [The time or circumstances alluded to in the verse] brings good to the world.

61. There are times and places destined for good, and the opposite is also true.

62. Sometimes a decree is forestalled by the Leader of the Generation, and sometimes by the people of the generation.

63. Through one's enemies, one can know the decree of Above.

64. When a man tells his suffering to a friend, the listener must act wisely at the time of hearing, so that the same suffering will not come upon him.

65. One who studies Torah in the night, the Holy One Blessed He draws upon him a thread of kindness in the day.

66. One must give money for a pidyon [lit. redemption. Money is given to a tzaddik who redeems the contributor from any judgments].

67. As long as you can be saved through money, do not use prayers.

68. When there is a disagreement Above on some matter, they rely [lit. support themselves] on the opinion of the Tzaddik in this world.

69. In the moment when a person is being judged above, they judge his name. Sometimes the messengers switch it with

Sefer HaMidot

another name, and through this the decree of death or hardship comes on someone else.

70. Someone who does not pra [lit. ask for mercy for his generation, through this he is punished.

71. Someone who has a sick person or pain in his house should go to a Torah sage, that he should pray [lit. ask] for mercy on his behalf, or that he [the Torah sage] should bless him.

72. When it is heard that someone is making accusations on the Jewish people, those who hear should speak aloud of the merits of Israel as show a meritorious interpretation of the actions that brought on the accusation, and it is necessary to strive to find merit.

73. When the Holy One Blessed He sees that people are zealous for His honor, through this He retracts His anger.

74. The primary pidyon or prayer is only in the in the day.

75. Not everyone is fitting to make a pidyon [redemption].

76. One who wants to sweeten dinim should not drink any wine the whole day.

77. With humility, one can find favor with the Holy One Blessed He.

78. When there is a din, pray with fervor.

79. Building a stone house entails danger of death.

80. Charity sweetens harsh judgment.

81. The immersing in a mikva sweetens harsh judgment.

Sefer HaMidot

82. After the passing of a decree, one needs to enclothe the prayer within stories.

83. Through the opening of a Torah scroll, judgment is sweetened, and it is settled in its place.

84. Through silence, the judgment is sweetened.

85. Fasting and sackcloth are conducive to annull an edict.

86. To sweeten the judgment, say the Torah portion concerning the eleven goatskin curtains [that served as roof for the Tabernacles - Shemot 26:7-14, 36:14-19], and the Ketoress [incense, there were 11 fragrances in the Ketoress - Shemot 30:34-38], the eleven blessings that Moshe gave to the tribes [Devarim 33:6-25], and the Chariot of Yehezkel.

87. And the portion about vows [Bamidbar 30] and mishnayot of the Tractate of Shavuot.

88. Through submission before GOD, a decree is annulled.

89. Through the Song of Songs, decrees are annulled.

90. One who is able to engage in Torah, and does not, suffering comes upon him.

91. The Tractate Ohalot [Tents - dealing with the parameters of impurity] is conducive to annulling decrees.

92. One who raises a dog arouses din.

93. Sometimes, the Holy One Blessed be He pushes a wicked person down into some hardship, in order that he go to the Tzaddik and ask that he [the Tzadik] pray on his behalf.

94. Sweetening the dinim is through casting lots, as with [the goat sent] to Azazel on Yom Kippur. The explanation of this

Sefer HaMidot

matter I heard from his [Rabbi Nachman] holy mouth, at the time when I wrote this before him: That one should take two coins, and cast upon them lots - one lot "to GOD", and one lot "to Azazel". The coin that on it came up the lot "to GOD" should be given to charity, and the second one that on it came up "to Azazel" should be thrown away or destroyed, and through this the judgment is sweetened.

95. Sometimes when the Tzaddik of the Generation with his anger that he is angry at you, he sweetens judgments.

96. When a new king arises among the nations or a new minister, then the din is aroused.

97. Through being stiff-necked against repentance, one brings on himself a great breakdown which has no healing.

98. It is not good for two people with the same name to dwell in the same home [lit. in one home].

99. Through depression, one arouses harsh judgment.

100. Through abashment the din is sweetened.

101. One should make known his suffering to the public.

102. When authority is given to a destructive angel, he doesn't differentiate between the righteous and the evil. Furthermore, he even starts with the righteous.

103. A change of place tears up an edict.

104. Through having mercy, one sweetens the din.

105. Sometimes a man dies from fear or some other sudden death, believe that this was his appointed time.

106. Through a lowly bearing, one can annul a harsh decree.

107. Through attending to tzaddikim, the judgment is sweetened.

108. In the merit of visiting the sick, one will not die as a culmination of suffering.

109. When the measure or attribute of din of Above reaches a man, even if it has not begun to take prevail over him, one can sense the measure or attribute of din through the flies that are in the house.

Part II

1. One who works to sweeten judgments, through this it will be easy for him to sanctify GOD's name, without prevention. Also, his eyes will not become dim.

2. Through suffering, crowns are made.

3. One who accepts suffering in order to lessen the suffering of the Jewish people, through this he will merit Divine Inspiration.

4. The portions on the festivals written in the [Torah] portion of Pinchas is conducive [segula] in through reading them to annul dinim, and they are conducive to triumph under the gentile legislation.

5. Through charity, one sweetens the judgments of the Time to Come, that is, of the Day of Judgment in the Time to Come.

6. One who knows, when he sees a din on Israel, to flip the din onto another nation, in the aspect of "and I will put a man in your place", through this all the creations return their power and become included in him - in this man, in order to renew their power. Also, through this the gate of various parables is opened in the world.

Sefer HaMidot

7. Those benefactors of kindness, who do kindness and sometimes cause - through the kindness they do - something bad, and they pretend they do not see the bad which resulted from their kindness. This is the aspect of the warning given to the Cohanim [priests] - who are the aspect of kindness - not to take large steps [end of the portion of Yisro, Shemos]. Through this, they cause the Judgment Above to be without deliberation. Also, the opposite: When they take particular care in their kindness, that evil should not result from it, through this the Judgment Above is with deliberation.

8. One who rebels [lit. kicks] against suffering is as if he says to GOD, "Leave me!"

9. When a man learns until he is exhausted, through this he sweetens judgments and arouses mercy. Also, through this, he arouses mercy for [lit. by] his father in the grave.

10. Appeasement of the Measure or attribute, of Judgment is not [can not be accomplished] with empty hands [meaning, it is necessary to spend money, whether it be charity, expenses for a mitzva, or destroying expensive items that are heretical].

11. One who was bitten by a dog, it is certain that GOD's mercy has been withdrawn from him. Also, it is certain that he has transgressed with eating forbidden foods.

12. Sometimes a man is hidden from the Measure or attribute of Judgment, with this that the Tzaddik exalts and glorifies himself over the man and casts him down.

Success

Part I

1. Anyone who gives his tithes properly does not lose

Sefer HaMidot

anything [to the tithing].

2. Join a successful person, and you will be successful.

3. Blessing abounds only on something that it is hidden from sight.

4. Success - assistance from Heaven brings it is.

5. Someone whose success has ceased and is not successful will not come to success quickly.

6. Immediately after Torah scholars there is blessing in the work of their hands.

7. Engagement in Torah is a segulah for success.

8. Someone who does not leave over bread on his table never sees the sign of blessing.

9. Since he only mentioned the one good side and not the reverse, this is not considered divining [The Torah forbids one to make readings of occurrences to decide what the future holds and how to proceed, whether or not to do something or in which direction to go. However, one is permitted to make for himself a one-sided sign of success, that such and such an occurrence will be a sign of success].

10. A house, child, and wife are omens for success.

11. Someone who divorces his wife will not be successful.

12. Someone whom the hour is fortunate for him, his heart is exalted, also the fear of him is cast on everyone.

13. Someone who does not speak unnecessary words is successful in everything he does.

Sefer HaMidot

14. Someone who always speaks the truth, he is successful.

15. Through confession, you will be successful.

16. Success comes to one who feeds a Torah scholar on his table. that is hosts him or possibly even, supports him. See also above.

17. When you do not have truth, success is taken from you and given to the gentiles [lit. the nations]

18. For success, listen when the Tzaddik recites the unification of GOD's Name, that is Shimma Yisroel [Hear Israel, GOD who is our GOD, GOD will be GOD for everyone, GOD is One]

19. Through faith in the sages comes success.

Part II
1. One who is always happy, through this he is successful.

2. One must honor someone to whom the hour is fortunate.

3. A successful person the [determination of success of the] time is in his hands.

Thoughts

Part I
1. Through humility, one is saved from thoughts of idol worship.

2. When you are praying and thoughts of idol worship befall you, concentrate on the name "Elo-hainu".

3. Good thoughts come through confession that is confessed before a Torah scholar.

Sefer HaMidot

4. Someone who tells stories that happened to righteous men, through this, good thoughts are drawn to him.

5. Someone who has bad thoughts, should judge everyone favorably always.

6. Through tears, all lusts become despicable.

7. Someone who does not believe in the Tzadik, as a result, his heart is not right with Hashem, may He be Blessed.

8. The belt that a Tzadik was girded with - when you gird yourself with it, it is conducive [segula]to nullify evil thoughts.

9. Through falsehood, the holy covenant [male's sexuality] becomes desecrated.

10. Someone who sanctifies himself, and pride arises in his mind, when he breaks the pride, he attains and acquires the Torah.

11. Crying out nullifies ulterior motives.

12. Learning the four sections of the Shulchan Aruch [Code of Jewish Law] nullifies ulterior motives.

13. Thinking about some Torah thought that you innovated is conducive to nullifying alien thoughts.

14. Someone who has bad thoughts should speak disgraceful words to himself.

15. Eating and drinking disturb the thought process.

16. Through anger comes thoughts of idol worship.

17. When one disparages the Festival holy days, he comes to having thoughts of idol worship.

18. One who sits among lewd people or in a place where there was lewdness, through this, he comes to evil thoughts.

19. The evil inclination only craves something forbidden to him.

20. Lusts - the loving-kindness of Hashem, may He be Blessed, is clothed in them.

21. Through pardoning of sins, you merit a clean heart.

22. Through compassion, lusts will be nullified from you.

23. Through the eyes, the heart craves.

24. Through the lusts of the heart, it is impossible that something impure will not cling to you.

25. Regarding thoughts of promiscuity, it is conducive to drink a laxative.

26. Prayer with heartfelt concentration opens all the openings Above.

27. Someone who has thoughts of idol worship should not carry with him any gold.

28. Through drunkenness, thoughts of idolatry come.

29. Through love for women, honor is taken away from you. Also, your wife does not grasp the seed, and miscarries, and at the time of birth, the child dies.

30. Through strife comes thoughts of idol worship. Also, a house in which there is strife will be a house of idol worship.

Sefer HaMidot

31. When foreign thoughts come to a person, he should raise his voice as if he were crying, and through this, the foreign thoughts will depart from him.

32. Through oaths and curses come bad thoughts.

33. Through having trust in GOD, evil thoughts will not come to you.

34. Grinding the teeth is conducive [segula] to nullifying evil thoughts.

35. According to the place in the prayer, so do the holy sparks clothe themselves in distractions and come to a person in order to be rectified.

36. Learning Tractate Yadayim [hands] is conducive [segula] to nullifying bad thoughts.

37. Someone whose prayer is only for the sake of the Divine Presence, will not have foreign thoughts come to him.

38. Through peace, His Name, may He be Blessed, is elevated.

39. When a man or woman thinks at the time of marital relations about some non-Jewish man or woman, and the thought is with love for that non-Jewish man or woman, then the child who is born from these relations will abandon the Jewish faith.

40. The ritual fringes are a fence, safeguard for lewdness.

41. Through visiting the sick, one is saved from the evil inclination.

42. The evil inclination does not rule except on what his eyes see.

43. Someone who reaches twenty years old and has not married a woman, all of his days he will have thoughts of sin.

44. Someone who commits a sin and afterwards thinks about doing more, even though he doesn't do it, is punished for the thought.

45. To push away the evil inclination, say, "The Merciful One berates the Satan [Rachamana nigahr bey baSatan]."

46. The coveting and evil thoughts which arise in the heart suddenly, which are not in a person's power to prevent, one is not punished for them, unless one repeatedly thinks about them.

47. For most bad character traits, it is good to bloodlet.

48. Through eating fish, lust is increased.

49. Someone who eats through the merit of his forefathers, thoughts of idol worship befall him.

50. Through homosexuality comes thoughts of idol worship.

51. One who thinks [sexually] about a Cuthean [non-Jewish] woman, comes to thoughts of idol worship.

52. One who looks at nakedness, his hardness becomes aroused.

53. One who belittles the Festival holy days, it is as if he worships idols.

54. Someone who has faith, the Holy One, Blessed be He, protects him from coming into the grip of bad thoughts, and he proceeds to That World to ComeAt the time that they are involved in Torah and acts of kindness, their evil urge is placed under their control. without sin, and the Holy One,

Sefer HaMidot

Blessed be He, helps him.

55. At the time that they are involved in Torah and acts of kindness, their evil urge is placed under their control.

56. Someone who has enjoyment from something heretical, he will eventually be compelled to idol worship.

57. When someone holds himself back from sins and seeks atonement, this causes that he will not even sin in thought.

58. Someone who has relations with a Cuthean [non-Jewish] woman, draws down filth unto himself. Afterwards, when he has relations with his wife and bears a child, the child will be an apostate.

59. A sash is a remedy for bad thoughts.

60. Someone who has thoughts of women, the way to nullify them is by not deceiving people.

61. Also, through charity.

Part II

1. When thoughts of idol worship come to a person, and he nullifies them by thinking of his faith in GOD, then his thoughts become an aspect of dew of blessing. Also, through this, his mind has fortitude and does not ever become confused; even when the mind becomes tired from pondering some deep concept, then the Holy One, Blessed be He, arranges for him thoughts which relax his mind.

2. Someone who guards himself from thoughts of idol worship merits to have constant faith [confidence in GOD], to the extent that he does not worry what he will eat tomorrow, and he is on the level of "Blessed is Hashem day after day." Through this, the Holy One, Blessed be He, perceives no wrongdoing and sees no iniquity in him, and

Sefer HaMidot

anyone who touches him, it is as if he touched the pupil of His eye.

3. Regarding thoughts of idol worship, one should rouse in one's mind and one should accept upon himself to get involved in acts of kindness, and through this, he will be nullified from thoughts of idol worship.

4. Through thoughts of idol worship, one's breath becomes shortened, and he derives no pleasure from good news.

5. When thoughts of idol worship come to a person, he should know that they are judging him Above.

6. Studying codifiers of Torah law nullifies thoughts of idol worship.

7. Through the establishment of unqualified judges, comes thoughts of idol worship.

8. When thoughts of idol worship come to a person, he should know that he will come to some illness or some accusation from a governing official.

9. Through thoughts of idol worship, one will ultimately need to make use of holy names.

10. Through tithing, thoughts of promiscuity are nullified.

11. Sometimes, it will arise in a person's thought that he will think about some illness. This is caused by Hashem, may He be Blessed, in order that he should remind himself to fix the evil thought which is the cause of that illness.

12. Thoughts of idol worship, thoughts of immorality, bloodshed and evil speech come to someone who is accustomed to making vows, but they become nullified by the leader of the city, who arranges the fines and taxes upon

Sefer HaMidot

each person, according to the amount that each one can handle.

13. When a person goes out to the market and is fearful lest he come to evil thoughts from what he sees, that he might see attractive women, he should recite the verse, "Behold, their brave one's angels cried out … angel of peace cried bitterly". Through this, he will be saved from seeing.

14. Someone who has thoughts of idol worship, should know that the hand of the nations of the world will reign upon him.

15. In a city that has fairs and big market days, there you will find many thoughts of idol worship. A segula for this is to toil in Torah on market days, and thoughts of idol worship will not come to him.

16. When one nullifies thoughts of idol worship, through this, all of his sins are forgiven.

17. Gazing to the east nullifies promiscuous thoughts.

18. Crying nullifies promiscuous thoughts.

19. The nullification of thoughts of idol worship comes through [holy] enthusiasm.

20. Through deception, one comes to thoughts of promiscuity with a non-Jewish woman.

21. One who has thoughts of having relations with a gentile girl, it is certain that he will experience some downfall, or his wife and children will get sick.

22. Through thoughts of idol worship, enemies come and become elevated over a person.

23. To nullify promiscuous thoughts, one should imagine the image of his father. Good advice regarding evil thoughts is to get mad about something. This is alluded to in the verse, "Rage and do not sin". I heard from our master, of blessed memory, that the intent is to rage and get angry at oneself. This is hinted at in the words of our rabbis, of blessed memory: A person should always enrage his good inclination over his evil inclination, as it is written, "Rage..", that is, to rage and get angry at oneself. But not to, GOD forbid, actually get angry, because the sin of anger is extremely grave, as is known. It is also a segula [conducive] to uproot from one's place and and go to another place. It is also good to jump from one's place.

Distancing the Wicked

Part I

1. When a tzaddik comes to the house of a wicked person, the house is blessed, but this is only when the house is fit to receive blessing.

2. Keep far away from the wicked, so that you will not be caught up in their punishment.

3. Due to enmity, one may come to display friendliness to the wicked.

4. Sometimes, when one does a favor for a totally wicked person, it gives satisfaction to the Holy Blessed One.

5. It is forbidden to relate their praise [evildoers]. However, in a case in which praising them will also result in praise for a tzaddik, it is permitted to relate a little.

6. One who judges a wicked one favorably is also called wicked.

7. Even when an evildoer does some act according to the

Sefer HaMidot

religious law, we do not depend on him.

8. One who was a guarantor for an evildoer, falls into sexual lust, and also becomes weak.

9. An evildoer who has forgotten GOD completely, it is certain that no upright descendants will issue forth from him.

10. When an enemy of GOD fall into your hands, do not have mercy on him.

11. When you do not attach yourself to liars, that are known to you, through this you will merit to discern the hypocrites.

12. One who hates enticers missionaries, their words will certainly have no influence [literally - stick] on him.

13. Through learning Torah, distance is created between the wicked who are drawing close.

14. One who distances himself from the wicked, the Holy Blessed One brings him a salvation.

15. The scattering of the wicked from each other is a sign of salvation.

16. Avoid living in a house in which an evildoer lived.

17. Do not speak to enticers missionaries, even to chastise them or bring them close to repent.

18. Associating with the wicked is damaging to the service of GOD.

19. It is appropriate and fitting for the holy servants of GOD to make a screen and shield, to the point that every afflicting and evil person will flee from it.

Sefer HaMidot

Part II

1. One who does not understand the wickedness of hypocritical evildoers is abhorrent.

2. Hypocrites cause eye pain to the errant masses who are fooled by them.

3. A man needs to guard himself from kissing evildoers, for the kiss creates a bond between them even after death.

4. There are those who are great apostates and heretics, but they do not reveal their heresy, and one is unaware of the need to guard himself. However, through the attribute of conducting oneself modesty, a person is saved from these heretics.

5. The wicked do not confuse us in our holy service through their sins that they transgress, as they do through the good deeds they do. It is for this reason that a non-Jew who observes the Shabbat is liable to the death penalty.

Pregnancy

Part I

1. Through falsehood, a woman has suffering in pregnancy.

2. It is beneficial [segula] for a pregnancy - that she carry on herself a small piece of wood from the roof over the grave of a tzaddik, or a magnet, and to give charity.

3. Small fish cause one to be fruitful and multiply.

4. Pregnant and nursing women should not eat garlic and onions.

5. A woman to whom the deeds of the wicked are hateful in

Sefer HaMidot

her eyes will, as a result of this, become pregnant.

6. Accepting exile upon oneself is conducive [segula] to pregnancy.

7. Eating the meat of small animals and drinking olive oil are conducive to pregnancy.

Part II
1. A woman who cannot conceive should look at the circumcision knife after the circumcision.

Seclusion

Part I
1. One who isolates himself and separates himself from others, they attend to him from Above.

2. Through isolating oneself and setting one's heart wantonly, one comes to anger.

Part II
1. The conversation that one conducts privately between him and his Creator, this conversation is made afterwards into a redemption and salvation for his children.

High Position

Part I
1. One who instills inordinate dread upon the public not for the sake of Heaven, does not see that is will not have a son as a Torah scholar.

2. One who begins a matter of a mitzvah and does not finish it, he is brought down from his high position.

3. When the Holy One, Blessed is He, takes retribution upon the enemies of Israel, He appoints for them directors who are not good.

4. The son of a righteous man is lifted to high position when he does not go in a straight path, in order that he should go in a straight path.

5. Through giving charity, one rises.

6. A man does not rise to high position unless he is forgiven for all his sins.

7. When Heaven raises an important man, they do not bring him down.

8. Through wisdom, humility, and being social, one's words are fulfilled above.

9. When Heaven wants to raise a righteous man and publicize him, Heaven sends discord between the evil people.

10. When someone humiliates you, and you accept it happily, through this you will merit respect and joyous eminence.

11. One who does not accept rebuke, through this he does not grow.

12. High position comes to one who constantly reviews his learning.

13. High position comes through rebuke.

14. One who Hashem his GOD is with him, he will have an ascent.

15. Through a change of name comes a change in fortune.

Sefer HaMidot

16. Through the traveling one does from village to village and from city to city, his words are not heard and accepted.

17. One who judges Israel favorably merits to a great ascent.

18. One who has high position, and fears lest he need die because his friend's time has come to receive this high position, he should flee from this high position, or he should employ a scheme that his friend should flee from this city.

19. When people come to one and say to him, "Teach us the Way of GOD", it is certain that he will have high position.

20. A man does not become famous, unless the Holy One Blessed is He appears upon him from above.

21. High position comes through having trust in GOD in time of trouble.

22. Someone with intelligence will certainly ascend to greatness quickly.

23. When the tzadik is raised to great height, everyone is in wonderment over him.

24. One who hates theft rises to greatness.

25. Through wisdom or success, one becomes famous.

26. A man to whom the nations of the world give him gifts, should know that his high position has been prepared correct or established by the blessed GOD.

27. Through saying Tehillim, one is elevated on high.

28. When a man attains high position, it is if he was newborn.

29. Due to mentioning names of idolatry, one does not rise or gain high position.

30. Through learning Aggadah [non legal lore of the Talmud and Medrash] at night, one rises.

31. Eminence comes about through hating falsehood.

32. Through loving the righteous tzadikim, one rises.

33. High position comes through spoken words or statements, insights, maxims, or the like.

34. Also, through submission before GOD.

35. Also, through submission before GOD.

36. Through sanctifying the name of GOD, one is raised high.

37. High position comes through having mercy.

38. Through faith, one rules over the arrogant.

39. One who appoints a judge who is not worthy will in the end be judged by [lit. fall into the hand of] gentile judges.

40. Through giving rebuke for the sake of Heaven, one merits to high position.

41. Through building a house in the Land of Israel, one merits to high position.

42. Through giving respect to the Torah, one merits to high position.

43. Not always can a man rule his domain for sometimes there comes a time which this time has vitality only from a different president.

Sefer HaMidot

44. Someone whom the Holy One Blessed is He has elevated, accord him respect and go to or be by him.

45. The ascent of a man is a goodness of the hour.

Part II

1. One who infringes his friend's territory, his greatness is diminished.

2. The Holy One Blessed is He does not give greatness to a man until He tests him with something small.

3. Through confusion of the mind, fear of GOD is ruined. Also, through confusion of the mind, one's dominion falls.

4. Through zeal, one merits to be a faithful leader [lit. shepherd]. A hint for this is in the passage, "Go to the ant, lazy one", and it is also written "From there the shepherd of the stone of Israel" the end letters of the words in this passage spell "ant".

5. When one bribes an official to be appointed to a position, that someone else should be removed and he should be appointed, this is like witchcraft.

6. Thoughts of idolatry, and promiscuous thoughts, and spilling blood, and slander come upon one who is accustomed to swearing oaths. However, they are annulled through the city's leader, who sets the collections and taxes on each person according to his worth, that he can bear.

7. When an evil person becomes great, it is difficult to bring out a new explanation in the rulings of the authorities of the halacha [Jewish law]. Also, the words of judges are not heard by the litigants.

8. A kosher man must humble himself when he sees the

sovereignty of an evildoer.

9. One who appropriates a position of authority for himself, through this his daughter becomes a prostitute.

10. One who leaves the needs of the community and engages in his own needs, is as if he takes bribery.

11. Through confession, one merits to high position.

12. Through the sanctity of the blessed GOD's name, the rule of the leaders of the generation has full power and might, and through this the mitzva of hospitality is highly regarded in everyone's eyes, and through this those that study the Torah merit that the Halacha [final legal ruling on a matter of the Torah] is like them.

Confession

1. Through confession, this causes The Holy Blessed One to bring teachers of children who teach faithfully.

2. This also elicits fixing of the roads from obstacles.

3. Through confession, one merits to leadership to be elevated.

4. One who does not confess his sins, fallen fear comes upon him.

Defers

1. One who is willing to defer to others, his sins will not be able to outweigh his merits.

Forger

1. Through forger comes the punishment of incarceration.

Sefer HaMidot

2. Through forgery, one becomes connected to the opposers of chasidus.

Ancestral Merit

Part I
1. Through immersing in a ritual bath, one's ancestral merit is remembered.

Part II
1. Brilliant, ingenious people of the generation inspire awe; through that awe, ancestral merit sparkles, and through the sparkling of ancestral merit, repentance is aroused in the world.

2. At the entrance to a man's house, it is discernible if his ancestral merit has finished, or if his ancestral merit is effective.

3. One who does acts of kindness does not need ancestral merit.

Memory

1. One who embarrasses his friend becomes forgetful.

2. Through worry comes forgetfulness.

3. Through learning aloud, one comes memory.

4. Through suffering one comes to forgetfulness from the heart, I was like a lost vessel - this can be translated and understood - I was like a vessel that loses-forgetsl.

5. By picturing before you the image of your father and mother, you will come to memory.

6. Through carrying out practical commandments, one is released from the measure of forgetfulness and is connected to the quality of memory.

7. Through promiscuity, one destroys the memory.

8. Through falsehood comes forgetfulness.

9. Someone without memory should bring people back in repentance.

10. Someone without memory, it is certain that he has not repaired the sins of his youth.

11. A forgetful person should give charity.

12. Someone without memory should sanctify himself with great holiness.

13. Through lowliness, you will merit to memory.

14. Through sadness comes forgetfulness.

15. One who keeps his learning hidden does not forget.

The Elderly

1. The elders uphold Israel, and their advice is good for us.

2. According to the elderly of the generation, so is the income.

3. If the elders are not wise, a sign of the matter is that their main esteem is by young women.

Sefer HaMidot
Zeal

1. Through zeal, one merits to be a faithful shepherd- leader of people. An indication of this matter: "Go to the ant [nemalla], lazy one" and the verse: "From there, the Shepherd, the Rock of Israel" [the last letters of this second verse spell out nemalla- ant, thus showing that the function of Shepherd is built on this quality of zeal].

Novelties of Torah

1. According to the novel interpretation that a person innovates in Torah, so is it drawn to him light - meaning inspiration and excitement, from the holiness of the Land of Israel.

2. Through "asmachtos" [lit. supports, this is a term used by the Talmud when a rabbinic ordinance is provided with some sort of basis from Scripture - this is explained in the continuation of this adage], abundant livelihood is bestowed upon the world. This is because there are many things for which we do not find an explicit verse from the Torah and our sages, of blessed memory, labored to find for them some sort of support So too in the matter of a livelihood, even if money wasn't explicitly promised, in the merit of the asmachtos, some type of basis is found to provide it.

3. Through novel Torah interpretations, the Providence of Hashem, may He be blessed, is more revealed to people.

4. When one of the children of Israel is incarcerated, through this, according to his aspect, the wellsprings of wisdom are concealed from the wise of the generation. The opposite is true when he is released from the incarceration.

5. Through novel Torah interpretations, there are additional converts.

Sefer HaMidot

6. When a person wants to attain any conception in Torah, then great accusation is aroused upon him. He is then in great danger, and needs to clothe himself in the visage of Abraham. He will then be saved from the accusation.

7. Torah innovators need to learn Torah codifiers before the innovation, and also afterwards. The study of the codifiers is a protection for the innovations, so that no stranger may touch them. Also, when a person wants to do charity, it is necessary to act the same way as with the innovations.

8. Novel Torah interpretations and charity - each one arouses one's friend.

9. According to the novel Torah interpretations, so are novelties innovated in the work of Creation.

10. Not every novel interpretation that a person innovates in Torah is permitted for him to write. For some are not given to write, even though they are given to expound. Someone who knows which are to be written, and which not, he will know and recognize one Jew among a thousand [thousands] gentiles [lit. from the nations].

11. A person needs to be careful not to speak words of Torah at a time and place when they will not be heard. Even at a place and time when they will be heard, it is necessary to weigh how many of them to say, so that he will not be in the aspect of "a fool emits all of his spirit". Because, through that, he brings about a disease called "geshvilleks" - swelling. Because this disease comes about through an overwhelming amount of water in the blood. And this is, "to make a weight for the spirit, and water He established in measure."

12. Through novel Torah interpretations, one merits a nice tallit - prayershawl.

13. The Tzadik toils towards some desire or some matter of the Torah to attain it. Afterwards, this thing comes to a lesser person without toil or labor. All this is because the door had already been opened.

14. When some wicked person becomes great, then it becomes difficult to innovate any reasoning in the [works of the] Torah codifiers. Also, the words of the judges are not acceptable in the ears of the litigants.

15. When one reveals a reason from the reasons of the Torah This term has an inference to the esoteric mechanism of the Kabbala, through this, the spirit of the people [lit. creations] are pleased or comfortable with him.

16. Those of little faith, it is difficult for them to conceive novel Torah interpretations.

Marriage

1. One who has difficulty finding his soulmate should say the Song at the Sea with concentration.

2. Kiddush Levanah - the Blessing over the New Moon. is a segula [conducive] to finding one's soulmate. A sign for this: The Hebrew word for moon - LiVaNA is the acronym for: "A virgin is married on Wednsday."

3. By making a marriage to a Torah scholar, benefits and blessings come to a person.

4. By making a marriage to a Torah scholar, one is saved from the punishment that comes through giving advice to do evil against a friend.

5. Through making a marriage to a Torah scholar, through these worthy judges are appointed.

Sefer HaMidot

6. One who has difficulty in finding his soulmate should accustom himself to reciting the passages about the sacrifices of the Princes of the Twelve Tribes.

7. A proposed match which is spoken about, even though the actual match is not completed, this is also from Providence, and the proposal itself has an impact on him and her.

8. The shroud which is used to cover the face of the bride before the marriage rites has the power of fertility.

9. Through prayer, one can change his soulmate that was announced in Heaven.

10. One who is careful not to spend the night or to live in a house; two couples in one house, through this he merits to have son-in-laws who are Cohanim priests and or very important.

11. When a man marries a woman after the death of his first wife, his first wife is anguished in the grave.

Dream

Part I

1. For a bad dream, say in the morning, "The dreams speak vainly."

2. For a good dream, say in a tone of wonderment, "Could it be that dreams speak vainly, when it is written 'In a dream I speak to him," describing the way GOD communicates with prophets.

3. One who conducts himself modestly in the lavatory his

Sefer HaMidot

dreams will be settled.

4. Through speaking disparagingly about a tzaddik who has passed away one is shown nightmares.

5. One who sees nightmares, it is a sign that a son or student will turn heretic in public [lit. burn the food he is cooking].

Part II
1. One who wants his dreams to be realized should write them in his ledger, and the day, the hour, and the place.

Favor

Part I
1. Through charity one attains favor.

2. Through humility one attains favor.

3. To find favor, one should be a host to guests.

4. Also, one should guard oneself from forbidden foods and guard one's mouth from forbidden speech.

5. One who expends money to acquire a rabbi from whom to learn, through this he will find grace.

6. When you defer, you will find grace.

7. Through giving rebuke, you will find grace.

8. Olive oil is a segulah auspicious for grace.

9. A segulah for finding grace is to write on parchment, "Silver and gold kindness and truth champion".

10. By the awe you have for a Torah scholar, you merit to grace.

11. Words that are spoken [lit. come out] calmly are accepted by people.

12. There are fish which are conducive to grace.

13. Learning Torah while traveling gives one grace.

Part II
1. When a man comes to a city to live, he should send meat to the poor of the city, and through this he will find grace in the eyes of the city's officials.

Flattery

Part I
1. Through adulation, one comes into the grip of foul language, and the opposite is also true.

2. Through adulation, one's wife becomes a widow, and his children orphans, and no one has compassion on them.

3. Through adulation comes fright.

4. Someone who walks in the marketplace and falls, it is certain that he has adulation in him.

5. Through adulation comes heartache.

6. Someone who relies on others, comes into the grip of adulation.

7. One who guards himself from adulation, through this, salvation comes to him.

8. It is permitted to adulate wicked people in this world.

Sefer HaMidot

8. Through adulation, judgment is aroused.

9. Also, one's prayer is not heard, and one becomes repulsive in everyones' eyes.

Part II
1. Through adulation, one comes into the grip of heresy.

Investigation

1. Contemplation of the world of chaos - that is, what is above and what is below… [concepts beyond our grasp] - causes curse. Conversely, one who guards himself from these investigations causes blessing.

2. Due to speculating about what is above and below… one's sustenance comes with great effort.

3. One who delves deeply into the subject of the Chariot - "merkava" a mystical Kabbalistic concept of the Divine Presence, passes away before his time.

Nature

1. Bodily health, one's life, and a person's nature all go according to the nature, life, and health of one's father and mother.

2. Someone whose hair is unnaturally abundant; this may lead to great damages and bad injuries from the Other Side. It is conducive for him to recite the section [of the Torah] that is read on Yom Kippur.

Purity

1. A kosher woman cleanses the house from leprosy.

Sefer HaMidot

Wandering

1. Through wandering, one merits a good name.

2. For the most part, the GOD fearing - their livelihood comes through having to go from place to place.

3. Sometimes the Tzaddik comes to wander, so that when he comes to the World to Come, he will remember all the places he had been, and through this, good will come to those places.

4. Not in every place does a person merit to have fortunate attainment of Torah and good deeds. For this reason, the Holy One Blessed He brings about circumstances causing the person to leave one place and go to another.

5. Sometimes a person is obliged to suffer exile, and it is switched for him to some sickness.

Lineage

1. The force of a curse does not affect one with respected lineage.

2. Even a righteous woman, if she does not have respected lineage, through this she will have children who are not upright.

3. It is difficult for the Holy One Blessed be He to cast away
and annul those with respected lineage.

Fear of God

Part I
1. Someone who is not wise in his own eyes is able to come

Sefer HaMidot

to fear of GOD.

2. Someone who draws close to an elder and withstands his anger, through this he merits fear of GOD.

3. When someone has the opportunity to do kindness and he does not bestow it, through this, he falls from his fear of GOD.

4. Someone who minimizes conversation will merit fear of GOD.

5. Someone who speaks and motivates his friend to fear of Heaven, all the words that leave his mouth at the time that he speaks with his friend get made into a book.

6. Someone who has fear of Heaven, his words are heard.

7. Crying over the death of a kosher person is considered like fear of Heaven.

8. Fear of Hashem increases for a person beyond what his mazal fortune mandates, and the opposite is also true.

9. Through serving righteous people, one comes to fear of Heaven, and the opposite is also true.

10. Shame leads to fear of sin.

11. The merit of fear of GOD lasts for a thousand generations.

12. Someone who does not leave behind a son or a student, this is called "not fearing Elo-him".

13. Covering the head brings one to fear of GOD.

14. A person from whom the populace is blessed certainly has fear of Heaven.

15. Someone who has fear of Heaven can break the heart of the haughty.

16. And draws down the Divine Presence into the world.

17. And comes into the grip of submission to GOD.

18. Also, the instigator is not able to deviate him.

19. One who constantly clings to the fear of Hashem, may He be Blessed, the Holy One, Blessed be He, does miracles for him.

20. One who is constantly connected to the fear of GOD and does not forget about it - all of his sins are pardoned.

21. One who has fear of GOD will certainly listen to the voice of the righteous.

22. He will also come to the attribute of trust in GOD.

23. Through fear [of Heaven] the Holy One, Blessed be He, gives him peace.

24. Someone who does not have fear of GOD, does not walk in the way of Hashem.

25. Through fear of GOD, one comes to truth.

26. One who has fear of GOD does not fall from his greatness, and keeps getting greater.

27. One who has the wisdom of Elokim [GOD] in his heart, the people will be afraid of him.

28. Someone who has fear of GOD, when fright comes to the world, he will not be afraid. Rather, he will even be happy.

29. Someone who has fear of GOD will certainly humble himself before the Tzadik.

30. Through haughtiness, there is no fear of GOD.

31. To acquire fear of GOD, go to the ritual bath.

32. Through sanctifying the Name of GOD, you will come to fear of GOD.

33. Intentional sins remove the fear of GOD from before his eyes.

34. Someone who does not pay attention to the day of death, through this, he has no fear of GOD.

35. When a person falls from his fear of GOD, it is known that they judge him Above.

36. Through the gift that one gives to the righteous, one merits fear of GOD.

37. Also, 310 immersions in a mikva [ritual] bath are a segula [conducive] to fear of GOD.

38. Desire, that a person desires to perform a Torah commandment - is a sign that he has fear of GOD.

Part II
1. Through fear of GOD and kindness, one is saved from fire and merits a livelihood.

2. A place of Torah decision [that is where the scholars study, decide, and teach the proper Torah conduct] is helpful for fear of GOD.

Sefer HaMidot

3. Through learning the Shulchan Aruch [Code of Jewish Law], one comes to fear of GOD.

4. Through the outstanding and sharp ones of the generation, fear of GOD is illuminated, and through fear of GOD, the merit of the forefathers is sparked, and through the sparkling of the forefathers, repentance is aroused in the world.

5. There is power in the hand of the individual to cast off the yoke of Heaven, but it is not within the hand of the masses to cast off the yoke of Heaven.

5. The voice that emanates from an intelligent, holy person is a **Segula** [conducive] to fear of GOD.

6. Through confusion of the intellect, fear of GOD is ruined. Also, through confusion of the intellect, one's authority falls.

7. Monetary interest causes a loss of fear of GOD.

8. Those who draw close to GOD fearing people, they also merit fear of GOD and knowledge.

Salvation

1. A miracle is only done for someone who has self-sacrifice to sanctify the name of GOD.

2. One who is joyous amidst suffering brings salvation.

3. Through hisbodidus [speaking to GOD in seclusion] comes salvation.

4. Through one's passing a test, a miracle is done for him.

5. Through charity comes salvation.

Sefer HaMidot

6. Through the modesty of a man, he receives in return, all the good that was taken from him by another through the other's prayers.

7. A miracle is not done for one who is promiscuous.

8. Do not depend on a miracle, as long as it is possible to be saved through money or other means.

9. Before the Holy One -Blessed is He- does a miracle for a man, the man falls into evil. completely according to the magnitude of the miracle.

10. One who does not mention names of foreign deities, the Holy One - Blessed is He- does him favors.

11. One who needs a salvation should give happiness to the Tzaddik.

12. Through trust, a man is saved and ejected from his troubles.

13. Through charity you will merit that you will not need salvation of man [that is through other people].

14. Through trust you will merit to understand that your salvation is from GOD, and not from man.

15. Also, through truth you will merit this.

16. When a person comes to a test, he should know that if he stands in it [that is not succumb to temptation], the Holy One, Blessed is He- will do a miracle for him.

17. Through trust, one merits to rejoice in the kindness of the Blessed GOD.

18. Through learning in a standing position, one annuls the scheming of the nations.

19. Through a fast, a man is saved from death.

20. Through having trust, kindness will be met out to you.

21. Through humility comes salvation.

22. One who prays joyfully will merit rejoicing in His salvation.

23. A miracle comes through truth.

24. A miracle comes through fear of GOD.

25. One who makes known the Way of GOD to the many, through this, even if he is amongst the gentiles, the Holy One -Blessed is He- saves him.

26. One who prays all day long through this he will merit to receive salvation.

27. When the Jews speak the truth, through this kindness is sent to them from Heaven.

28. Through the melodies that you sing, you arouse the Holy One -Blessed is He- to look upon the nation whose melody you are singing - why it subjugates you.

Honor

Part I
1. When there is a desire to discourage a man from serving **GOD**, they give him honor in order to distract him.

2. One who speaks against the Tzaddik ends up humiliated in everyone's eyes.

Sefer HaMidot

3. One who belittles himself each day in his own eyes, merits that his name will not be forgotten by the people, and people will name their children after him.

4. Tikkun Chatzot [the Midnight Lament or Rectification] is a segula [conducive] for honor.

5. One who causes the Blessed Holy One's glory to be raised high, he becomes famous.

6. One who offends the honor of tzaddikim, through this he falls into weakness.

7. Hugging the Torah scroll is a segula [conducive] for honor.

8. Through humility comes honor.

9. Sometimes a man receives honor and greatness because of the merit of one of his household.

10. One who says "I did not sin" is despised in everyone's eyes.

11. Most of the humiliations that come upon a man are due to the sins of his youth.

12. Extraordinary thirst is a sign of descent from honor.

13. One who saves a Torah scroll from any danger of destruction merits to honor.

14. The words of an honored man endure.

15. When you give honor to a man, give honor also to the one serving him.

16. When the dead are unearthed, it is certain that the Holy

Sefer HaMidot

One, Blessed be He, wanted to bring some humiliation on the living, and the matter was overturned.

17. One who transgresses the command of the Tzaddik, he falls from his importance.

18. Through chasing after honor, one comes to idolatrous thoughts.

19. A man with a position of importance, it is not necessary to [that is one should not] humiliate him, even if he is wicked.

20. It is necessary to give honor to the monarchy, even though he worships idolatry.

21. Through the honor one gives to the Torah, one is saved from his enemies.

22. A miracle's honor is in its coming discreetly.

23. One who is despised, it is certain that he likes falsehood.

24. A man's clothes give honor to the man.

25. Honor is dependent upon the soul.

26. Honor is dependent upon the desire in the heart.

27. If you are being pursued - attacked, you will merit to have honor in this world.

28. Through visiting the sick, everyone is honored with him.

29. One who gains prestige by the shame of his friend will not merit to a book named after him.

Part II
People who honor each other, it is certain that they are

upright, and so too the opposite.

2. All the honor of all the monarchies in the world, are included in the Four Monarchies. Through the fashioning of the Menorah, **Kiddush Levanah** [Sanctifying the New Moon], the Incense, and guarding oneself from forbidden foods, all Four Monarchies return the honor within them to the Blessed Lord.

3. By going forward to honor an important man, the ten utterances by which the world was created are aroused. This also comes through bringing those who are distant back to GOD.

4. It is necessary to honor one who the hour fortune smiles upon him.

Sorcery

1. Children who are born through incantation of names of impurity or through sorcery will grow up to be sexual offenders.

2. And all who involve themselves with the names of impurity, he can be damaged by anything.

3. Sorcery only harms those who are haughty.

Anger

1. One who guards himself from anger, those who hate him have no dominion over him.

2. Also, he will dwell in his house, and others will not lodge in his place.

3. Through anger, one is humiliated.

Sefer HaMidot

4. Do not lose your temper and you will not sin.

5. Anyone who becomes angry; his wisdom and prophetic ability departs. And even if greatness has been decreed for him in Heaven, he is brought down from his greatness.

6. The Holy One Blessed be He loves one who does not become angry and one who does not harbor resentment.

7. A hot-tempered person's life is not worth living.

8. Also, all sorts of hell reign over or afflict him.

9. And is overcome with hemorrhoids [in the shape of figs].

10. The Divine Presence is not important to him.

11. And it is certain that his sins are more than his merits.

12. And increases stupidity.

13. And it is certain that his sins are more than his merits.

14. Anger after eating is very damaging.

15. The anger of a woman destroys the house.

16. Through anger one's flesh becomes emaciated.

17. It is conducive for avoiding [or possibly: calming] anger, to eat bread in the morning.

18. One who does not complain about people will be esteemed in peoples' eyes.

19. Through falsehood comes anger.

20. One with a bad temper should make a pledge and pay it

Sefer HaMidot

immediately. Through this the anger will be annulled from him.

21. One who gazes at the face of a liar comes to anger.

22. Through jealousy one comes to anger.

23. Through anger one incites upon oneself harsh judgments.

24. Through anger one sires foolish children.

25. Through anger, one's lifespan is shortened.

26. It is conducive to [dispelling or preventing] anger, that you lower the haughty.

27. When you don't have anger, through this you will be able, with your gaze, to humble the arrogant.

28. One who has a bad temper, it is certain that he loves honor, and even all the commandments [good deeds] he does, he only does for honor.

29. One who is angry at an honorable pauper, it is as if he taunted GOD.

30. Also, he becomes mute.

31. And becomes a leper.

32. One who breaks the vice of anger will merit a good name.

33. Sometimes anger comes through [bearing] a heavy burden.

34. Through anger comes depression.

Sefer HaMidot

35. Anger comes through hisbodidus [seclusion] not carried out appropriately.

36. Through choler, there is no peace.

37. Through eating, anger departs.

38. Guard yourself from anger on a day in which you had a salvation.

39. Through giving charity, anger is annulled.

40. Through anger, a woman has difficulty in childbirth or having children.

41. Anger frightens a person.

42. Anger damages eyesight.

Learning

Part I

1. One who gives delight to his father and cheers him, through this he will have desire and love for learning.

2. When you want to give life to something through reciting words of your Torah, do not expound on negative subjects. Rather, expound on verses and subjects that deal with the good.

3. When a man recites novel Torah teachings, through this he gives joy to the Blessed GOD.

4. When a wicked person says Torah, know that he causes to stumble those who listen to his teaching.

5. One who causes his friend to desist from his learning, it is certain that he has deviated from the Way of GOD.

6. Torah learning, even while half a sleep, is good.

7. Through accepting suffering with love, one does not forget his learning.

8. All the Torah that a person tried to learn in this world, and was prevented from understanding the full true intent of the learning, he will merit to understand it properly and truthfully in the World to Come.

9. Through rising for a Torah scholar, one merits to Torah.

10. All the knowledge one gains in the laws of the Torah, whether dealing with the commandments relating to one's fellow man, or those between man and his Creator - the knowledge itself is a success for the soul.

11. A book written with ink made from olive oil is conducive [segula] to learning.

12. Awe of a Torah scholar is a segula [conducive] to learning.

13. One who engages in Torah at night, the Divine Presence is before him.

14. What should a man to do gain wisdom, He should increase in learning yeshiva [lit. sitting], minimize business, and ask for mercy. Because any one of these without the other is not enough.

15. Speaking in a loud voice brings feeling and movement to all the limbs.

16. One who learns in a loud voice lives long, and he retains what he learned [his learning is upheld in his hand].

17. One without arrogance, he retains his learning [his learning is upheld in his hand].

18. Also, one who teaches others.

19. Hearing directly from the sage is more beneficial.

20. Learning Torah is greater than offerings of the Tamid [sacrifice brought twice daily in the Temple].

21. One who says, "This Torah saying is pleasant, and that one is not" loses the wealth of the Torah.

22. Relearning something forgotten is harder than learning something new.

23. One who forgets one detail from his learning causes the exile of his children, and he is brought down from his greatness.

24. A Torah scholar who's inner being does not match up to his outward appearance is called an abomination.

25. A Torah scholar - the citizens of his city are obligated to do his work.

26. Due to annulling Torah study, GOD is made, so to speak, poor [that is put in a position where He is unwilling to help].

27. Torah study is greater than saving lives, and building the Temple, and honoring one's parents.

28. Through holiness one merits to understanding.

29. There are three over whom the Holy One, Blessed is He, cries every day, and one of them is a person who could engage in Torah and does not.

Sefer HaMidot

30. Through understanding, one merits to repentance.

31. It is forbidden to teach a wicked man a wondrous matter.

32. A great man can learn from the wicked, but a simple [lit. small] man can not.

33. Regularity of learning rises above the keeping of all the commandments.

34. One who is without a wife languishes [lit. is soaked or permeated] without Torah ad good.

35. One who learns by himself cannot compare to one who learns from a rabbi.

36. It is not pleasing to the Holy One, Blessed is He, when the Jewish people are judged unfavorably.

37. One who loves a Torah scholar, he and his seed will remain steadfast in Torah.

38. A person should learn even if it is without understanding.

39. It is very beneficial to see the mouth of the rabbi during the learning.

40. It is very beneficial to learn near rivers.

41. One who engages in Torah at night is as if he is engaged in the service in of the Holy Temple.

42. One who studies the laws of the Temple Service, it is as if the Holy Temple was rebuilt in his days.

43. One who teaches Torah to an unfit student falls into Hell, and is as if he were casting a stone to the idol - marcolis.

Sefer HaMidot

44. The Torah itself was given to all of Israel. But pilpul [formulating and developing argumentation and disputations] was only granted to Moshe alone, and he, in his generosity, gave it to all Israel.

45. When a man gives himself over entirely [hefker] to teach the Torah to all, the Torah is granted to him as a gift.

46. The Torah one learns is only preserved by one who impoverishes himself for her by abstaining from any business, and by one who makes himself as if without knowledge.

47. Learning precedes fear of sin, and fear of sin precedes in-depth study.

48. Through eating bread in the morning [pas shacharis], one's learning is preserved, and one merits to learn and teach.

49. Torah study must specifically be recited aloud, for the learning which is only in thought is forgotten, and does not come to be actualized in deed.

50. One who learns but does not review is comparable to one who sows but doesn't harvest.

51. One who reviews his learning - the Torah requests from GOD to reveal to him the taamei Torah [lit. the taste or cantillation or reasoning, with an inference to the esoteric] and its secrets.

52. One who does not have established times for learning comes to promiscuous thoughts.

53. One who does not review his learning has difficulty raising children.

54. One who learns Torah for its own sake creates peace in

Sefer HaMidot

the pamalia - gathering of the wise, often translated as tribunal, Above and Below, and protects the whole world, and is as if he built the Upper and Lower Palace, and hastens the Redemption.

55. One who teaches his friend's son Torah, is considered as if he created him, and as if he created the words of Torah, and as if he created himself.

56. One who blackens his face for the words of Torah in this world, GOD will make his face radiant in the World to Come.

57. One who goes hungry for the sake of learning Torah, GOD will satiate him in the World to Come.

58. One who reads books of apostates is considered an apostate [lit. is called an apikorus].

59. One who reads a scriptural verse in its time brings good to the world.

60. When there are two verses, from one you can expound on merit and good, and from the other you can expound on the opposite, expound on the verse which is of merit and good.

61. One who does not have understanding in his learning should spend a Shabbat with a tzaddik. Also, through this he will merit to learn Torah for the sake of Heaven. Or he should endeavor to do some favor for a tzaddik, or learn with joy, or bring in the Shabbat with joy, or greet the tzaddik with joy.

62. Through learning in-depth, one is able to pray.

63. One who cannot learn because of impediments should abstain from intoxicating beverages.

64. Through neglecting Torah study, one comes to neglect prayer, and this is also the case in the converse.

65. One who cannot learn due to lack of time, and he learns on Shabbat and Rosh Chodesh [the first day of the month], with this he closes off the spirit of impurity.

66. When one does not understand one's Torah learning, it is certain that harsh judgments are laid upon him.

67. It is easy to understand some concept when one is in a high location, such as on a mountain or other such place.

68. Arousal in the morning to study is conducive [segula] to the sense of hearing.

69. Through teaching the Tinokos shel bais 'Raban - very young children, peace proliferates.

70. It is necessary to pray that one will merit to have upright students.

71. Through expounding on the Torah in a positive light, one can bring salvation.

72. Through an expansive heart, one can understand one thing from another.

73. One who has no desire to learn Torah should not speak about anyone any bad word.

74. Do not learn, except by someone who is Heaven fearing.

75. Through Torah, you will merit peace.

76. When you say Torah [ideas developed from the Torah] according to your level, and not beyond it, through this GOD will honor your commands.

Sefer HaMidot

77. Due to blasphemy, a person does not have desire to learn.

78. Through giving charity for the sake of the Divine Presence, one merits to Torah for the sake of the Divine Presence.

79. Through getting up at midnight, one merits to understand the Torah and explicate it.

80. One who interrupted his Torah study for trivial matters, his rectification is to get up at midnight.

81. One who hates falsehood as he would an abomination, he will have passion to learn.

82. A book that a wicked person learned from, do not learn from it, for the letters of the book will make you wicked.

83. When you hear Torah or moral instruction from someone, and in you heart you gain no respect for him, it is certain that he is a fool.

84. Torah learning for which you incur expenses, through this it will not be forgotten from you.

85. One who chases after the desires of his heart, through this you will find him alluded to in all the passages of the Torah - disparagingly.

86. One who separates himself from the Torah connects to the Satan.

87. Two Torah scholars who honor each other in legal study for the sake of the Divine Presence, and in humility, GOD grants them success, and they rise to greatness, and merit to the Torah that was given by GOD's right hand, and merit to things given through the right hand of the Torah.

Sefer HaMidot

88. A Torah scholar who avenges and is spiteful like a snake - cling to him, for in the end you will benefit from his learning.

89. It is forbidden to learn from one who is drawn to idol-worship, and one who learns from him is liable to the death penalty.

90. Torah learning without deeds is like myrtle, which has fragrance but no taste.

91. By whom do you find orders of Torah [that is vast arrays] By one who rises early and stays up late for them in the study hall, and blackens his face for them as a raven, and makes himself cruel as a raven [regarding the needs of] his children.

92. A person cannot merit learning from anyone. Because of this people travel great distances to learn.

Part II

1. There are sufferings that come upon a person, whose allotted time is according to the alignment of the stars that determine all such sufferings. However, through the desire and longing that is aroused in students at the time appointed for their study sessions with their rabbi, through these sufferings are annulled before their appointed time.

2. The Torah, the tithes, and the Shabbat give physical life as well as spiritual life.

3. Through learning the Shulchan Aruch [Code of Jewish Law], one comes to Fear of GOD.

4. One who learns Torah with a pure mind - that his eating is holy to the point that he is nourished from the food that the angels from. Through this his enemies are punished with strangulation. This is learned from Torah passages: "And it was on the third day, at the beginning of the morning", "And in the morning there was a layer of dew", "And it was in the watch of the morning".

5. Through the outstanding and sharp ones of the generation, fear of GOD is illuminated, and through fear of GOD, the merit of the forefathers is sparked, and through the sparkling of the forefathers, repentance is aroused in the world.

6. Learning poskim the works of those who determine the halachah Jewish law annuls thoughts of idol worship.

7. When one goes from master to master, then he needs to strengthen his faith in the Unity of Hashem, may He be Blessed. Because learning from many teachers damages faith in the Unity. So too, the master who has faith in the Unity, he is able to illuminate to each and every student according to his ability, and each student only hears what he needs, and no more.

8. A teacher who teaches his students in this manner - that is, he only teaches to each student what he specifically needs to hear, not more and not less. Through this he merits that the most pleasant and praiseworthy aspects of the Torah are revealed to him.

9. When a student hears words of Torah from a rabbi, and annuls his will to the will of the rabbi, according to this you can be sure that he listened. For when he does not annul his will, even though he hears, he really does not hear. Also, when his feelings [senses] are annulled at the time of hearing, this is a sign that he has truly heard.

10. At the time when a student comes to hear Torah from a rabbi, the student's evil - that is, the impure husks [klipos] created by the evil in him, also come to hear and draw from it. However, when each student hears only what is relevant to his soul, as was described above, the evil spirits [klipos] flee, and are not able to hear. Yet there is a subtle evil [klipa] which is close to holiness, that will only flee when there is within the Torah teaching a message of salvation of Israel, then it also flees. A hint for this from Scripture: "And Moshe sent his father-in-law" - if one learns this passage according to the opinion that Yitro [the father-in-law of Moses] came and went his way before the giving of the Torah.

11. One who utters words of Torah is saved from the sentence of stoning.

13. A man cannot merit to Torah and good deeds in all places. Due to this, GOD brings about circumstances that cause the man to go from one place to another place.

14. When a man learns until he is exhausted, he sweetens judgments and arouses mercy. Also, through this he arouses mercy for his father in the grave.

15. Through Torah, one comes to Faith, and through Faith, one comes to sanctify the Name of GOD.

16. Those with pure eyesight can recognize in a man, who is the rabbi who taught him Torah. This is specifically when the one looking is familiar with the face of the rabbi. For through the religious law that a man learns from his rabbi, his face becomes similar to the appearance of the face of the rabbi, for the law is his wisdom that enlightens the face of a man [as in the verse, "The wisdom of man enlightens his face."] When one receives the law, one receives an aspect of the appearance of the teacher's face. And according to the number of laws he learns, the more aspects of the appearance of his face are acquired.

17. Through sanctifying the name of GOD, may He be blessed, the authority of the leaders of the generation is in full force and strength. Through this, everyone values the commandment of hospitality to guests, and through this, the Torah students' merit that the law is set according to their opinion.

18. One who is strict with others and lenient with himself, and says about what he did not hear, that he heard, due to this, he does not merit to see the beauty of the King. For the evil force [klipa] of Edom, which is negative fear, darkens the light of his eyes, so that he cannot see the beauty of the Face of the King.

Mockery

1. Through mockery, one will have many creditors, and they will rule over him. Also, he will fail in promiscuity. Also, his wife will dominate him.

2. Through mockery, one walks and falls [alt. - continuously falls]. Also, he comes to falsehood, and wandering from place to place.

3. Through adulation comes mockery.

4. Through mockery comes suffering.

5. Through mockery he does not have wisdom.

6. Mockery makes a person loathsome to GOD and to people.

7. Through mockery come fires [lit. burning].

8. One who mocks the words of the Sages is judged or sentenced to be committed in boiling excrement.

9. All forms of mockery are forbidden, except for the mocking of idol-worship.

10. Mockery is a dreadful matter - for it begins with

suffering and its end is annihilation.

11. One who mocks, his sustenance is diminished, and he falls into Hell, and he brings destruction to the world.

Slander

Part I

1. One who slanders, the Holy One Blessed is He says to the Official of Hell, "I am on him from above, and you are onto him from below." His remedy is to engage in Torah and humble his self opinion. Also, through this he will not come to slander.

2. Through slander, one enlarges his sins to the proportion of the three sins [that is the three most serious categories: Idol-worship, sexual sins and murder].

3. A matter said in the presence of the person being discussed, or in the presence of three listeners, are not accounted as slander.

4. This slander, even though it should not be accepted outright as true, it warrants suspicion.

5. One who speaks negatively about the People of Israel, in the end he will be have illness on this mouth.

6. When there is not love between the Jewish People, gossipers are made, and through gossipers, scoffers are made.

7. People who love one another, it is permitted for them to tell each other things they heard from someone else, and the one who hears is permitted to accept his words, and this does not constitute slander.

8. Through slander, a man does not have desire to learn

Sefer HaMidot

Torah, also he derides the Tzaddik.

1. From slander one is saved through truth.

2. When one guards himself from slander, he will also not contemplate bad on his fellow.

3. One who does not accept slander about a Tzaddik, through this he will merit to be counted among the tzaddikim.

4. Coarseness brings a person to speak disparagingly about others.

5. Slander, one doesn't say until one comes to denying the core of faith and sinning in the Heavens and earth.

6. It is permissible to say slander about one who causes strife.

7. One who says false slander on his fellow [lit. lets out a bad reputation - based on a lie], he doesn't ever get forgiveness.

8. Through slander, one cannot receive the countenance of the Divine Presence.

9. One who says slander, and one who listens to it, it is fitting to thrown hm to the dogs.

10. A rectification for slander is the recitation of the [passages describing the] incense-offering.

11. Due to slander, plagues [This might refer specifically to leprosy] come upon him, and his sins are magnified till the heavens, and it is fitting to stone him.

Part II
1. Through slander, one is caught and incarcerated.

Sefer HaMidot
Circumciser

1. One must seek out a mohel who is a tzaddik and Heaven fearing. For when the mohel is not good, it is possible that the child he circumcises will be unable to sire, GOD forbid. Also, when the mohel is not good, through this the child can come, GOD forbid, to falling sickness [epilepsy].

2. A woman who is unable to conceive should gaze upon the circumcision knife immediately following the circumcision.

3. The mohel gives the circumcised child understanding in the learning of the Torah.

4. The commandment of circumcision has the power that resides in the clothes of the Cohen Gadol - High Priest.

5. One who is born circumcised, it is certain that his power of imagination is good and proper.

6. One who does acts of kindness, the name that he bestows will endure. For this reason, before naming a child, one should do kindness, and through this the child's name will endure.

Money

Part I
1. One who ridicules - his livelihood is diminished.

2. The speech - terminology of the sages brings wealth.

3. Wealth does not endure, on account of not having mercy on people.

4. One who stands in a test of sexual immorality will merit to great wealth amidst his enemies.

Sefer HaMidot

5. Great is work, being that GOD warned about it, that a person should do some type of work.

6. Weak people such as ourselves, should borrow in order to eat.

7. One who wants to become wealthy should deal in small animals [Like sheep and goats] in a remote location.

8. The amount a person spends on eating and drinking should be below his means, and he should dress and cover himself according to his means, and he should honor his wife and children beyond his means.

9. Poverty in a man's house is harder than fifty plagues - like those of Egypt.

10. A man's wife does not die unless others ask him for money and he does not have it.

11. The power that the non-Jewish nations have to steal from Israel comes from their studying the Scriptures.

12. Wine brings poverty.

13. A man who has cognizance, in the end becomes wealthy.

14. One who steals from his fellow-man, through this they make him impure with the impurity of subconscious emission.

15. When some new understanding comes to a man, it is certain that great wealth is at [lit. attached to] its heel [The commentators don't provide any citation, so I suggest - when they are guarded there is a great reward at its heel, but when there is a slip up, who understands - so when they are guarded there is understanding and great reward at its heel].

Sefer HaMidot

16. Money of a Jew that falls into the hands of a gentile, immediately becomes permissible [that is another Jew can salvage the money for himself].

17. One whose sons and daughters are enduring famine; through this he is spared from the judgment of burning that is one of the four death-sentences of the religious courts.

18. One who disregards the safeguards the Rabbis established to protect the Torah becomes poor.

19. One who overcomes his lust of eating, merits to a nice abode.

20. A man's livelihood is paramount to the splitting of the Red Sea, and more than the Redemption, and twice as difficult as childbirth.

21. Whence a person is appointed as a parnas [president to manage the welfare] of a group, he becomes wealthy.

22. The Incense burned in the Temple makes [the officiating priest] wealthy.

23. A person should not worry saying, so-and-so curtailed my livelihood. For against their will seat you in your rightful place and call you by your rightful name.

24. On account of four things, the possessions of householders fall into continuous reduction: For delaying the payment of employees, for fully denying employees their salary, and for casting off responsibility from their necks and placing it on their fellows, and for arrogance.

25. Changing one's place and name are beneficial for making a livelihood.

26. The rain is only withheld due to not giving terumos portion for priests and tithes, people who speak lushon hura - bad talk or slander, haughty people, annulling study of the Torah, and the sin of stealing.

27. A rectification for lack of rain - make abundant prayer.

28. Through faith, livelihood is abundant.

29. When there is prosperity [lit. satiation - antonym of famine] in the world, physical weaknesses are diminished.

30. The rain is only withheld due to those who publicly pledge charity and do not give.

31. Disgusting things or actions in the house bring poverty.

32. Three things bring a man to poverty: **1.** One who urinates in front of his bed, naked, **2.** One who is careless in ritual handwashing, and **3.** One whose wife curses him in front of him.

33. Giving tithes is conducive [segula] to wealth specifically in the Land of Israel.

34. Honor to the Torah and honor to the Shabbat is a segula [conducive] for wealth.

35. The kezayit - measure like that of an olive, of bitter herbs that is eaten on Passover, is a segula [conducive] for wealth.

36. Writing a Torah scroll is a segula [conducive] for livelihood.

37. A daughter of a Cohen marrying a common Jew, or a daughter of a Torah scholar marrying an unlearned man, brings him to poverty.

Sefer HaMidot

38. Joining forces with one whose fortunate hour is at hand is good for success.

39. One who loves GOD in the midst of his eating, drinking and other pleasures, merits supporting many nations.

40. One who despises money merits length of days.

41. One who searches after treasures brings his time of death closer.

42. One who has not rectified the sins of his youth becomes impoverished.

43. One who exhausts himself day and night for an income, and does not attain it, his rectification is to bring others back in repentance.

44. One who breaks some vessel unintentionally, it is certain that he is a sinner.

45. One who is enthusiastic or bent, to work the land, certainly he is of no benefit.

46. In everything you do, ask the Tzaddik to pray on your behalf.

47. Constant joyfulness is conducive [segula] for success.

48. Derech Eretz - trade or occupation. needs encouragement or strengthening.

49. One who includes GOD in his pain, his income is doubled. Also, his income flies to him like a bird.

50. Through the sin of neglecting terumos [portion given to the priests], and tithe-giving, profit is lost, and people run after their income and do not attain it.

Sefer HaMidot

51. Rain is given in the merit of individuals, and income is given in the merit of the many. But an individual whose merit is great is considered like the many.

52. Through the kiddush made over wine, rain comes, and his prayers are heard.

53. One who keeps his father's Torah scroll in his house merits wealth.

54. Rain comes in the merit of one man, one field and one blade of grass, and in the merit of the land, and kindness, and suffering.

55. The rains are withheld due to idol worship, and because of promiscuity, and due to a Tzaddik who was not eulogized according to law [that is befittingly], and due to those who diminish the income of others.

56. Through poverty, one is spared from the punishment of Hell.

57. Through using holy names, come poverty and death, and even to someone who is able to protest it and does not.

58. When someone is in a position that he should be screaming out against his fellowman who is stealing from him even jeopardizing his food, but is silent, GOD does justice for him.

59. When a man sees that his food income is limited, he should give part of it to charity.

60. Worry and strain over his income, food diminishes the strength of a man.

61. Through sexual immorality comes poverty.

62. Sometimes when a tzaddik has no fortune with respect to income, opposers are brought up against him, and through this, he is given the income that was intended for them.

63. One who is involved with construction becomes poor.

64. learned from the adage of our Sages, he who wants to become wealthy should aim his prayers northward, the word for north can also mean to be hidden, which can be understood as modesty, thus establishing this entry.

65. From the time that stingy people began to proliferate, there was a proliferation of those curtail the income of others.

66. The sustenance of a person is diminished when he does not judge others with the benefit of the doubt.

67. Also, when he mixes water with his drinks.

68. Also, when a person listens to the advice of a tempter.

69. Also, when one commits a sin in order to anger GOD, he becomes poor, and the world does not believe him that he is poor.

70. One who deals with impure names and witchcraft becomes poor - The commentators do not provide a citation here, a possible hint can be from the verse - a sorcerer do not let live - which can also be read, will not live, which we find elsewhere in the teachings of our Sages means that the person will become poor, who is likened to the dead.

71. When the sickness of weakening of the flesh, which is called Dar, comes upon one of the members of one's household, it is an omen of poverty.

72. When some shame comes upon a person, it is an omen of poverty.

Sefer HaMidot

73. One who despises money, he is taught from Above the way he should go.

74. Sometimes the death of karet [dying early due to certain sins] is replaced with poverty.

75. A poor person is confused like a drunkard.

76. Through overcharging [According to a possible root of this dictum, this word can be translated as verbal abuse], one becomes impoverished.

77. One who conducts his affairs in haste, with an unsettled mind, falls into debt.

78. One who curtails the livelihood of another is as if he murdered him.

79. A man should always hold fast to the estate of his forefathers, and not sell or exchange them.

80. One who desires money, he falls from his level.

81. Through apostasy comes poverty.

82. One who is poor should strive to provide food to those who beseech GOD.

83. Faith is good for livelihood.

84. Pain in the eyes is an omen for poverty.

85. Through submission, a man's livestock increases.

86. Through charity, one merits to a livelihood.

87. One who gives money to sorcerers causes that his livelihood will be dependent on a gentile household.

Sefer HaMidot

88. The words of the Tzaddik bring income.

89. Depression causes loss of income.

90. Through giving charity, you will have expansion.

91. A lot of sleep brings a person to poverty.

92. One who involves himself in Torah and charity merits wealth.

93. Esteem your wives so that in that way you become wealthy.

94. Blessing is not prevalent in the house of a man except for the sake of the honor of his wife [therefore a man should be diligent in honoring his wife].

95. One who lends on interest, his possessions collapse and do not rise.

96. Through the annulling of irreverent music, prices are lowered.

97. One who has no livelihood should study Torah and afterwards pray for a livelihood - certainly his prayer will be accepted.

98. A man should not sell the first item he purchased.

99. One who intrudes on the livelihood of his fellowman is called an evildoer.

100. No man would come to hurt his friend, if not for the arrogance in his heart.

101. Crumbs are conducive to poverty.

102. A wealthy person is the aspect of male, and a pauper is the aspect of female.

103. Pain in the eyes is a sign of damage.

104. For all attainments, whether it be wisdom, wealth or children, one must engage according to the laws of nature, but ask for mercy from GOD, that he be successful in the matter of his engagement.

Part II
1. A year which is a year of business is a good sign for physical health.

2. One who is passionate about working the land, comes to one of three things, either, spilling blood - that is murder, or leprosy, or drunkenness.

3. Through fear [of Heaven] and kindness, one is saved from fire, and merits a livelihood.

4. When Torah arbitration decreases, through this income decreases, and so too the opposite.

5. Through the finding of Torah sources for Rabbinic traditions, large income is delivered emanated, into the world. This is because there are various things that we don't find a reference to them in the Scriptures of the Torah, and the Sages of blessed memory labored to find them some sort of basis.

6. Sometimes GOD brags about the upright of the nations in front of the Satan, so that He can give livelihood to Israel without accusation.

7. Through the longing with which a person craves to be buried in the land of Israel, through this comes great income.

Sefer HaMidot

8. For a feast of a mitzva a person should take the trouble even to chopping wood. When splitting the wood, he should have the intention that he is splitting and separating out the evil from the good in the Tree of Knowledge. Through this he will merit to a livelihood.

9. Through repentance, livelihood comes easily.

10. One who fulfills the maxim, "Your friend's money should be precious to you like your own", through this he merits to pray with intention in his heart.

11. Great is one who benefits from the exertion of his hands, for he recognizes the honor of GOD what angels don't know.

12. According to the changes that are done by the angels - for example, sometimes they are sitting, sometimes standing, sometimes they are female, sometimes male, and other such differences - so the bounty that comes from Heaven varies; sometimes fire, sometimes water, sometimes stone, and so other endowments. All these variations are manifest in the world and in man. Also, the will of a person changes according to the variations - sometimes he wants one thing, and sometimes he wants something else.

13. A person's livelihood is according to his marital match.

14. According to the elders of the generation so is the livelihood.

15. Interest monetary detracts fear of GOD.

16. One who lends on interest cannot find anyone to judge him favorably.

17. One who guards himself from transgressing the command not to envy, through this he is saved from anger, arrogance, and lack of faith that comes in the wake of anger and arrogance.

18. Through faithful business conduct, curses are annulled.

19. One who needs to borrow from others, he is comparable to an animal.

20. Someone who is a middleman, when he wants to intercede, in order that an important man will buy an item from a common man, and he sees that his words are not being accepted by the common man - to sell the item to the important man, in that case the broker should pray that his words have effect on the common man, and he will sell to the important man.

21. One who controls his evil inclination, his children will not become delinquent or involved with bad society or culture. Through this his money will be blessed, and through this he will not come to be tested.

22. Traveling [lit. thoroughfares] brings a person to lushon hura [evil speech], idol worship, promiscuity, and spilling blood that is murder, and these sins detract one's livelihood.

23. Through the money one gives to the poor of the Land of Israel, through this one's money is preserved in his keeping.

24. Fires [lit. burning] come to the world on account of money used for idol worship, to destroy it.

25. When a new king or a new minister arises, livelihood is renewed and undergoes change.

26. One who has dealings and business with non-Jews at the time of their festivals, or even not at the time of their festivals - but his revenue is from supplying things for their idolatry, through this his wife has bleeding shortly after her ritual immersion.

Sefer HaMidot

27. One who makes a separation between a man and his wife - that is, he goes to the man and praises his wife to him, but goes to the wife and defames the husband in her eyes, until a separation is created between them - he becomes troubled, preoccupied, overtaken, by his expenses for food or sustenance.

28. One whose merchandise and estates are scattered, and not in one place - sometimes he is saved through this from having to tear his garments for his deceased.

29. The largest businessman in a city is the light [lit. candle] of the city.

Informer

1. One who informs on his fellow man [to gentiles] ends up being a vagabond, enemies rise up against him, he experiences himself that which he wanted to bring upon his fellow, all those who depend on him fall, and the family of the one he pursued takes his greatness.

2. One who informs [to gentiles] on the Tzaddik loses all his possessions.

3. It is permitted to kill an informer [to gentiles].

4. It is forbidden to deliver [to gentiles] even an evildoer to execution.

Famous

1. There are famed leaders whose fame is mainly created through dispute.

2. A person is tested in order to make him great and famous.

Sefer HaMidot

3. Through strife, it happens that the lesser students become famous before their time. This is the aspect of miscarriage, that the infant emerges into the air of the world before his time. This causes poverty, and sometimes causes deaths, GOD forbid.

Miscarriage

Part I

1. Due to fear, a woman miscarries.

2. A segula [conducive] for one who miscarriages with stillborns, is that she should carry with her a magnet. Also, she should carry with her a piece of wood from the grave of a tzaddik. Also, she should give charity.

3. A woman who is prone to miscarry should carry with her dew-water.

4. A segulah [conducive] for one who miscarries, is that she should sell her fetus.

5. On account of the sin of needless hatred, a woman miscarries stillborns.

6. Through her lust for food and drink, she miscarries.

Part II

1. A woman who miscarries stillborns should not go with golden jewelry.

2. The grinding of flour and kneading of the matzah of Passover is a segulah [conducive] that miscarries with stillborns.

Sefer HaMidot
Contention

Part I

1. There is no maintaining a stand in war as a result of the transgression of an oath.

2. One who pursues his fellow-man [to attack or harm him], GOD brings evil upon him [the pursuer] in order that he will forget his fellow man from pursuing him.

3. Through the recitation of Hallel [six specific chapters of Tehillim traditionally recited together on certain holidays] the Holy Blessed One will save you from your enemies.

4. Through giving honor to the Torah, a man is saved from those who hate him.

5. Before engaging in war, it is necessary to pray to the Blessed GOD.

6. Each time that a person falls from his faith, he draws upon himself a rich and powerful adversary.

7. When a person prays about his enemies, he should pray in the morning.

8. Gazing frequently at the heavens, this annuls the hatred of one's enemies.

9. When one forgets the poor, he does not triumph.

10. A poor man that is pursued by an evil man, know that the poor man is arrogant.

11. One who is obsessed with winning, the Holy Blessed One forgets him and hides His face from him.

12. When a person is in distress, his enemies rise.

Sefer HaMidot

13. One who is obsessed with winning comes to forgetfulness.

14. Contention befalls a person when the person is presented with the opportunity to do a mitzvah, and he dismisses it and does not perform it.

15. One who quarrels with the Tzaddikim, it is certain that his thoughts are evil.

16. Sometimes location causes a person contention.

17. Someone who has enemies should humble himself, and through this GOD will save him from his enemies.

18. When a person has enemies, and he searches in all sorts of ways to find a way to love them, through this they will be as absolutely nothing.

19. When a person has enemies and he does not think of how to take revenge against them, but remains bound to the joy of the Blessed GOD, through this the Holy Blessed One gives him the power to avenge himself against them.

20. Those who sin sexually, for the most part, are fighters with that is against the tzaddikim.

21. When there is the trait of yielding humility, through this there is no fear at war, as if he is dwelling in an impregnable fortress.

22. One who is obsessed with winning is visited with incurable illnesses.

23. Two who are quarreling and take their case before a gentile dignitary, through this the Holy Blessed One brings upon them a blow that cannot be healed.

Sefer HaMidot

24. Sometimes, the Holy One, Blessed be He, hardens the heart of the wicked in contention against the righteous in order that the wicked, have a downfall.

25. One who gives honor to an elderly man is saved from war.

26. One who recounts his quarrel before the Holy One, Blessed be He, sees his vengeance on his enemies.

27. Through strife comes poverty.

28. One who quarrels with his neighbors ends up being an object of ridicule to his enemies.

29. One who is denigrated and remains silent is called pious and the Holy One, Blessed be He, guards his soul.

30. Fiery prayer, so fired up that it comes to his face, through this his enemies fall and are singed.

31. One who is good and upright from his youth, through this, when he has a conflict, many people will volunteer and band together with him to help him.

32. One who entices his fellow man and bars him from the good path, cannot stand up against his enemies in the time of contention and war.

33. Through confession, the thoughts of your enemies directed against you will be annulled.

34. A contentious person, it is certain that he likes sin or crime.

35. One who is reticent, no man can overcome him or compete with him.

Sefer HaMidot

36. When those opposed [to Chassidus -an approach to Jewish observance brought into the world by the holy Ba'al Shem Tov and his students] oppose chassidim and want to arrest them from their devotions of Heaven, through this they fall and become despicable in their own eyes.

37. For victory, say the chapters which opens, "On the eight-stringed instrument..."

38. One who visits the sick, the Holy One, Blessed be He, does not hand him over to his enemies.

39. One who has enemies should say prayers and petitions all day, and his mouth should not cease from prayer and supplication, through this the Holy One, Blessed be He, will save him, and his enemies will be shamed.

40. One who is pursued will merit having children and grandchildren.

41. One who has enemies should request of many people that they pray for mercy for him, and he will have peace from his enemies.

42. When you have enemies below in this world, it is certain that you also have enemies Above in the Upper World.

43. Through learning Torah, one's enemies retreat.

44. By having trust, enemies will not be able to harm you.

45. By having the trait of submission, your enemies will fall into the trap that they prepared for you.

46. One who prays all day - through this shame comes upon his enemies.

47. One who harms [lit. did bad to] the enemy of a tzaddik will merit to always triumph.

48. When people speak bad about you, learn Agaddah [legends of the Oral Torah] every night.

49. Two tzaddikim cannot live in the same city, until they have truth.

50. Through having trust in GOD, one's enemies will not rejoice in one's troubles.

51. One who does not humiliate his fellow man, his enemies will not rejoice over him.

52. One who has many enemies, it is certain that their hatred is not justified. For it is impossible that they are all vindicated in his wronging them.

53. When a man has enemies, and afterwards one of his own friends and comrades also rises against him, it is a sign that his opponents will stumble and fall.

54. One who has faith is not afraid from enemies.

55. Through prayer crying out from pain, one's enemies will not rejoice over him.

56. One who has enemies and does not know whether or not he will fall into their hands, should examine whether he falls from his level in service of the Blessed GOD, then it is certain he will be delivered into their hands.

57. For abating contention, learn the Tractate Sukkah.

58. Contention comes through an association of evildoers.

59. Due to depression, even your friends will oppose you.

Sefer HaMidot

60. Contention is not found or prevalent, in one's home only when all the produce in the house has been consumed.

61. Sometimes, when many tzaddikim oppose one tzaddik, the Holy One, Blessed be He sides with them, even though the truth rests with the one tzaddik. the other tzaddikim draw the Will of GOD to them.

62. One who calls his fellow man wicked, it is permitted to interfere with his business and to decrease his income by up to one third.

63. If a person does not have friends and those who love him, death would be relief for him.

64. All things are created in the aspect of male and female. Even kings - there is a king whose aspect is male, and there is a king whose aspect is female. The Holy One, Blessed be He distances them from each other, that they should not come to destroy the world.

65. One who is contentious, even if he is an intellectual knows how to study Torah, do not honor him.

66. In the place of contention; there is the Satan.

67. One who fulfills the commandment to recite the Shma, every morning and night, will not be handed over to his enemies.

68. Through learning Torah and performing kindnesses, one's enemies fall before him.

69. Through being pursued, a person becomes fit to be a sacrificial offering before GOD.

70. One should always side to save those being pursued or attacked.

Sefer HaMidot

71. The world would not continue to exist except for the sake of one who shuts his mouth at the time of contention.

72. One who forgets one detail from his learning causes antagonists to rise against him.

73. Through strife, that there is opposition on the Tzaddik, wars are aroused.

74. When people speak about a person, the evil inclination has power to strengthen himself over that person, and one must pray for mercy about this.

75. One who has difficulty accepting appeasement is from the feminine world.

76. For contention; go early and stay late in the hall of study and learn Torah. Or if it is impossible to bring those opposing you to judgment, in a Beis Din - Jewish court, pray about them, and the Holy One, Blessed be He, will knock them down, but do not hand them over to a [non-Jewish] official.

77. One who has cause to retaliate against his friend and remains silent about it, the Holy One, Blessed be He, does justice for him.

78. Do not contend with a man who is stronger than you, even though he drives you to do something dishonorable. However, if he has fear of the governor, go with him to an official, and do not do the dishonorable thing.

79. Through evil speech tale bearing, one loses falls in war.

80. One who refrains from speaking slander [tale bearing - lit. evil language] triumphs.

81. One who was accustomed to review Torah and then separated [ceasing his study of the Torah], through this

his enemies will pursue him.

82. When a man's wife bleeds outside of the time of her period, it is certain that some hatred has been aroused against him.

83. When the tzaddik has a conflict with someone and can save himself through monetary means, he should do so, and use his merits [lit. righteousness].

84. In all perpetrators of conflict, there are sparks from the souls of Dusun and Aviram [It is interesting to note that in the introduction to the holy book Aderet Eliyahu on the Holy Zohar, by R' Eliyahu Baal Shem Tov, he writes about how a group of people banded against him, just like Korach and his crew, and maybe some of them were from his reincarnation].

85. Conflict between two tzaddikim is for the good of the Jewish People: Know that this is true for also Above, there are two angels who are also in conflict, and there is no one to adjudicate for them except for the Holy One, Blessed be He, Himself.

86. One who hears his degradation and remains silent through this great evil that were fit to come upon him are nullified.

87. The Holy One, Blessed be He, always assumes a position in favor of the majority. However, if the majority is [comprised of] evildoers, He does not favor them.

88. One must not give the benefit of the doubt, interpret his actions in a favorable manner, to an inticer [someone who tries to bring people to foreign beliefs].

89. When there is a conflict between two people, and each one has people taking his side; when from Above, death is decreed upon one of the disputants, GOD forbid, it first

Sefer HaMidot

affects the supporter with the least stature, and not with the person who is the main contenders.

90. Sometimes it is decreed on a man that his seed will be wiped out. However, when he is delivered into his enemies' hands, the decree of the destruction of his seed is annulled.

91. One who distances a man from the service of the Blessed GOD causes that man to have descendants who will afflict the descendants of the one who distanced him.

92. One who has the ability to protest the deeds of the wicked and does not, it is as if he himself did the wrong.

93. One who sustains a conflict transgresses a negative commandment and it befits him to become a leper.

94. One who challenges the Kingship of the House of David is fit to be bitten by a snake.

95. Through being involved in studying Torah, one can withstand the vicissitudes of war.

96. One must strengthen oneself against those who hate him, and wage war upon them cunningly, and know that the Holy One, Blessed be He, will do what is right in His Eyes.

97. In situations of conflict, it is auspicious [segula] to say the passages, "And Asa called to GOD …" until "mortal." [Chronicles II, 14:10].

98. One who does not put his trust in GOD, through this he is confronted with war and conflict.

99. Through the study of Torah, fear falls upon the nations that they do not wage war against Israel.

100. In situations of conflict, say, "And he [king Yehoshafat]

Sefer HaMidot

said, GOD of our forefathers," until "For our eyes are turned to You." What was said by Yehoshafat by Yehoshafat.

101. In a time of war, one must prepare the weapons of war appropriately, and the Holy One, Blessed be He, will do according to His Will, but do not rely on miracles.

102. One who establishes a fixed place for his prayer, his enemies fall beneath him.

103. One should not pray for the death of any man, even an apostate. For it is better to kill them by mortal means, rather than by the Hand of Heaven.

104. Do not provoke an evildoer, all the more so [don't start up with] one whose hour of fortune is at hand [lit. the hour is laughing for him].

105. It is permissible to not admit the truth, and even deny it, in order that people not be led astray after an evildoer.

106. Due to baseless hatred, a person will have great conflict in his house.

107. Blows from a sword and great plundering come through the sin of procrastinating justice, distorting, and ruining judgment, and for neglect of Torah study.

108. A woman at the end of her menstrual period who passes between two men causes strife between them.

109. A pursued or attacked, person who placates the pursuer, through this harsh judgment is aroused upon the pursuer.

110. One who gives sustenance to his enemy causes a decree of burning on the enemy.

Sefer HaMidot

Part II

1. Talking bad about a tzaddik causes [heretical] philosophy to gain strength in the world, and so too, the opposite that is praising a tzaddik.

2. There are famous religious leaders whose fame is primarily created through controversy.

3. Through strife, one falls into sexual lust.

4. One against whom many arise to challenge him on account of his faith; and he stands up against them and makes well-received counter-claims, through this he will merit having many children, and the world will be filled with his seed.

5. One who always sets his mind's eye to investigate the leaders of the generation, examining them unfavorably [lit. with a "bad eye"], through this he falls into the hunger predicted for the future, that is to say, "...not a hunger for bread..." For the Hebrew word for hunger, Ra'AV, is the word RaV, with the letter Ayin [which is Hebrew for "eye"] in the middle.

6. Through giving charity, one defeats his enemies through minimal means or cause or effect, and the Holy One, Blessed be He, saves him from even the great means of his enemies.

7. By saying Birkat HaMazon - the blessings after the meal which fulfill the Torah mandate, "You shall eat, be satisfied and bless the Lord, your GOD...", the Blessed GOD becomes known in the world. Also, through Grace After Meals, the government is rested from strife and war.

8. One who's Torah learning is with a pure mind, including that his eating is so holy that he is nourished from the same food from which the angels are nourished, causes that his enemies be punished with strangulation. A sign or hint to the veracity of this matter is: three similar Biblical phrases -

Sefer HaMidot

"And it was on the third day, at the beginning of the morning…", "And in the morning there was a layer of dew…"", "And it was in the watch of the morning…".

9. The suffering and accusations that come upon a Torah sage cause him to forget.

10. Quarreling causes that students of small stature become famous before their time. This is an aspect of miscarriage - when a fetus comes into the air of the world before its time. This causes poverty, and sometimes even causes deaths, GOD forbid.

11. Sometimes a man does not have peace in his house, and all the members of his household quarrel with each other. It is certain that there are demons in the house causing all this - and though this affliction comes upon his household.

12. Sometimes a person's place causes him quarrels for the same reason as it is forbidden to ask about a person's peace in an unclean place. The Hebrew word for peace, "shalom" is a Name of GOD and should not be spoken in a filthy place - thus we find that certain places are contrary to peace.

13. Through pain and sadness, contention comes to the world. Conversely, through joy, peace comes to the world.

14. Revelation of the Torah comes through peace.

15. The business or work that a man strains to do on a fast-day, this matter saves him from enemies and murderers.

16. One who has enemies has difficulty concentrating in prayer.

17. One who causes a separation between a man and his wife - that is, he goes to the husband and glorifies the wife in his eyes, and then goes to the wife and discredits the husband in

Sefer HaMidot

her eyes, until it causes a separation between them - causes difficulty with his own livelihood.

18. When the Holy One, Blessed be He, sees that there is a tzaddik who has the power to draw people to the service of GOD, He raises up enemies against him inorder to enable him to draw people close to GOD. For a tzaddik without enemies cannot draw anyone close - just like in the days of the Messiah the world will dwell in tranquility, and then no new converts will be accepted.

19. Due to idolatrous thoughts enemies come and dominate [lit. elevate over] a person.

20. One whose enemies rise up against him falls into lust for food.

21. When a person feels itching in his body, he should know that he has enemies. Sometimes through the blows and bruises he brings upon his own body, he is saved from enemies, for one is in exchange for the other.

22. There are two tzaddikim, one of whose words are in plowing, and the other's in harvesting; or one whose words erect the bris [circumcision - a holy reference to the male covenant] for relations, and the other's words draw the seed and create the fetus in its mother's womb, and cultivate it. Thus, when there is an argument between these two tzaddikim, an outsider should not involve himself in their words that they speak one on another, in order no to ruin the goal.

23. One who has enemies should prohibit himself from wine, and through this he will become their head, that is leader or ruler.

24. A segulah to be saved from one's enemies - whether they are enemies in controversy or enemies on the routes of travel

Sefer HaMidot

– of whom he is afraid; is to say all the names of the ta'amim [incantation notes] of the Torah - that is: Pashta, Munach, Zarkah, etc.

Messiah

1. Through the stories of tzaddikim, the light of the Mashiach is drawn into the world, much darkness and suffering is dispelled from the world, and also one merits to attractive clothing.

2. Through repentance, the Spirit of the Mashiach wafts upon the harsh decrees of the nations [lit. kingdoms] and annuls them.

3. In the future, there will be a generation in the world that will be totally righteous.

4. Through Truth, the End of the exile, will come.

5. Through keeping the Shabbat, one draws upon oneself the light of the Mashiach, also through repentance.

Beverages

1. Through theft, drinks spoil.

2. Also, through arrogance.

Music

1. When tzaddikim are publicized in the world, through these new melodies are brought into the world.

2. The Leviim had a special melody designated for each day, but now, in the Exile, the melodies have been forgotten. When some tragedy comes upon some nation, the melody of the Leviim corresponding to that crisis is aroused [lit. sparks or glistens].

3. Through the melodies that contain a tone of crying, it is possible to release the captives, the aspect of "He brings out prisoners bakosharot [in a kosher, propitious time]." [The word bakosharot is split into two words by the Medrash: beki - meaning crying, shirot - meaning song - song with a crying tone].

4. Through song, a person can be discerned if he accepted upon himself the yoke of Torah.

5. That which a person when he drinks begins to sing and make melody or music, which is not so when he eats - this is because they [the Jews in the desert] expressed shira song of praise and gratitude to GOD over the Well, and not over the Manna.

Menstrual Impurity

Part I
1. A woman who bleeds abundantly is an excessive talker. She should not beautify herself in people's eyes, also she should wash in spring water, also she should not exert herself excessively. Also, her husband should be careful with ritual hand washing. Also, she should not get angry. Also, after her immersion she should give charity. Also, her husband should learn the tractate Nidah [Menstrual Impurity], and afterwards recite the Song for the Day [every day of the week has a different Psalm]. Also, she should wash herself with things that can be raised from nets in the river. Also, she should drink goats' milk. Also, she should wash herself using goat feathers, and smoke herself in frankincense.

Sefer HaMidot

2. A woman who is oozing blood should write the letters **lo echad** [not one], and carry it on her.

3. A woman who is immodest, through this she does not have a set time for her period and bleeds abundantly.

4. A woman in her time of impurity, who saw blood by chance, it is because of a sin of the husband.

Part II
1. A woman who does not have a period should fast.

2. A segula [conducive] to restore to a woman her period, is through hospitality.

3. One whose business and dealings are with the non-Jewish nations at the time of their festivals - or even not at that time, but he derives an income from supplying them with articles to be used for their idol worship - through this, his wife bleeds immediately following her immersion.

Deriving Benefit From Others

Part I
1. When a tzaddik accepts money from a wicked person, even if the money is possibly stolen, it is permitted for the tzaddik to accept it, so that the wicked one will not take on some wicked Torah scholar, claiming that the scholar is a tzaddik, giving him the money, and he will oppose the True Tzaddik.

2. Since the proliferation of those who accept gifts, days have become diminished and years shortened.

3. A person whom you have once received benefit from, do not humiliate him.

4. One who throws his weight around on the Jewish people

Sefer HaMidot

ends up being needy of others.

5. One who does favors for others is permitted to benefit from them, and they ought to serve him.

6. Through the benefit you receive from your fellow man, through this you suffer pain due to his sins.

7. One who does not accept money from others, will raise all his seed [the Hebrew word for raise or bring up, can also mean will make great].

8. The King funds his expenditures from the people.

9. One must be involved in some form of business, in order that ultimately, he will not need arrest the study of [lit. words of] Torah.

10. One who asks for his portion verbally is as if he had stolen.

11. One who is reliant on his friend's table, his world is darkened, and his life is not considered life.

12. One who has a neshamah [Jewish soul] is able to enjoy from smell.

Part II
1. Great is the benefit from the work of one's own hands, for it saves a man from killing.

2. One who hates [accepting] gifts does not fear from false accusations.

Sexual Immorality
Part I

1. One who entertains thoughts of a gentile woman, through

Sefer HaMidot

this his children will not be Torah students.

2. The fortune of a woman goes according to the fortune of the man, that is her husband; present or future - according to a source cited.

3. Intercourse that takes place in a beautiful home draws a beautiful and proper appearance upon their children.

4. He who has relations with a non-Jewish woman is considered as if he married her.

5. Perfumes inject desire in a man.

6. A daughter of a Cohen and a common Jewish man, or a daughter of a Torah scholar and an unlearned man - their match does not have fortune: Either she will be widowed, or divorced, or childless, or her husband will bury her, or she will bury him, or she will bring him to poverty and shame.

7. A promiscuous elderly man - people [lit. cognizance] cannot bear him, and eventually he becomes despised in his own eyes.

8. There are seven that are like they have been excommunicated, and one of them is one that does not have a wife.

9. Sexual desire can not be distanced from a man except through distancing the vision of the eye and thought.

10. Do not enter into negotiations with your temptations, for the elaboration of the sensations of the contemplator, even directed at negation, will affect reinforcement of the desire, and his will - will be overturned on him or towards it.

11. Through wine comes about most promiscuity.

Sefer HaMidot

12. One without a wife is not a man, and is as if he spills blood and diminished the image.

13. One who detracts from his wife's time - that is the time and circumstances that the Torah allows for procreation, and she suffers from this, is punished with death.

14. Sometimes, through marital matches whose partners are not suited to each other, one of them dies.

15. One who marries a wicked divorced woman, she comes to bury him.

16. The licentiousness of the wife destroys the house.

17. Anyone who has immoral sex, through this their wives see in a dream impurity called murrin.

18. Anyone who marries a woman for the sake of Heaven is as if he gave birth to her.

19. Through a marriage which is not holy comes fire.

20. Anyone to whom an opportunity to sin comes, and he refrains, a miracle is done for him.

21. One who marries a woman who is not appropriate for him, is as if he plows the whole world and plants in it salt, and when GOD basks His Divine Presence, He testifies on behalf of all the Tribes, but not on behalf of him.

22. One who breaches the Covenant - that is, one who commits sexual transgressions, is as if he transgressed all the commandments.

23. Pants atone for sexual immorality.

24. Through promiscuity, the righteous fall.

Sefer HaMidot

25. Through lamenting the death of the righteous, one breaks himself from love of women - that is: one breaks from himself the love of women.

26. Through spilling one's seed wastefully, one creates klipos, husks - evil forces, that enclothe themselves in people who oppose him, and antagonize him, and cause him suffering.

27. One who has relations with a married woman, in the end comes to spill blood - that is murder.

28. One who eradicates sexual transgressors, with this he rectifies the sins of his forefathers.

29. One who wants to guard his sexual purity [lit. the sign of the covenant] should always say the truth, and also should do kindness to one from whom he does not expect repayment.

30. For the rectification of despoiling sexual purity [lit. covenant], he should pursue peace.

31. Through strife, one comes to despoiling sexual purity [lit. covenant].

32. Promiscuous thoughts come as a result of the "Breaking of the Vessel of Kindness", and according to the abundance of fallen sparks, so is the abundance of the promiscuous thoughts.

33. One who transgresses the prohibition against homosexual relations through this he is caught and incarcerated.

34. Mercury is conducive for masculine might Euphemism for an erection.

35. One who has relations with his wife in a time of hatred,

Sefer HaMidot

the children born make themselves apostates.

36. Through promiscuity, one becomes exiled under the hand of frivolous governors, and becomes in-debt.

37. In the merit that the women guard against promiscuity, the Messiah will come, also a person will not be dependent on his fellow, and the honor of the tzaddikim is aggrandized.

38. Promiscuity comes as a result of involvement with names of the impure, that is names of impure or evil spiritual entities, and witchcraft.

39. One who has relations with a non-Jew [lit. a Kutite] channels all the bounty to the Other [Impure] Side.

40. Through promiscuity comes forgetfulness.

41. A repair for releasing seed in waste - that he should make efforts to bring people back in repentance.

42. One who guards sexual purity [lit. covenant], even if he does not have ancestral merit, the Holy One - Blessed is He, grants him merit.

43. Through inadequate faith come promiscuous thoughts.

44. Through the sin of witchcraft and promiscuity, the Tzaddik passes away.

45. The offspring of sexual offenders will become in need of witchcraft.

46. Offspring born through witchcraft will be promiscuous.

47. Sexual offenders, for the most part, oppose the righteous.

48. One who spills his seed in vain, it is as if he brings his

Sefer HaMidot

children as a sacrifice to idol worship, and also, he is judged by stoning.

49. Through promiscuity, one destroys the memory.

50. Through promiscuity, sense of shame departs.

51. Through overeating, one comes to promiscuity.

52. When a man commits a sin, afterwards he is pained due to the spark of holiness within him. But when a man violates his sexual purity [lit. covenant], he is not pained afterwards, for the spark has already left him.

53. One who does not despoil his sexual purity [lit. covenant], through this he has memory.

54. Promiscuous thoughts come as a result of false oaths.

55. Someone who serves as a guarantor for a wicked person becomes promiscuous.

56. One who destroys his path, Euphemism for wasting seed through this the wallet is penniless.

57. Through sexual immorality comes murder.

Part II
1. Through promiscuity, one falls into incarceration or to the sickness of feet pains. Also, a student who has not achieved, the level, of instructor, in Jewish law, and even still goes ahead, and rules, suffers this fate, also destructive spirits dominate him.

2. Through discord, one falls into sexual lust.

3. Through sexual relations on days that relations are forbidden, through this one falls into imprisonment.

Sefer HaMidot

4. Through sexual lust comes constipation, and from constipation comes leprosy.

5. Through favors one does for others, sexual lust is annulled, and so the opposite.

6. Guarding sexual purity [lit. the covenant] is the source of the blessings.

7. All who guard their sexual purity [lit. covenant] merit to understanding the seventy languages that are hidden in the Torah.

8. It is forbidden to judge favorably one who has transgressed with homosexual relations.

9. Parnassa [livelihood] is according to the marital match.

10. An unoccupied man who is not involved in any occupation, through this his sexual desire abounds, and he constantly speaks filthy words.

11. Someone who guards his sexual purity [lit. covenant] is permitted to rejoice when he sees the fall of his enemies.

12. Danger on the roads comes as a result of sexual impurity [lit. violation of the covenant]. A hint for this from the Torah: "my going and resting you have encompassed [meaning - have complete knowledge and control] etc." [these Hebrew words can also be translated as my seed you have scattered - thus hinting that by the scattering of one's seed, that is sexual impurity, one's travel will be endangered].

13. A woman who is accosted for sex, even if she did not actually have relations, the request itself leaves an impression upon her.

14. One who shuts his eyes to avoid seeing evil, through this he is saved from humiliations.

15. Through forbidden sexual relations comes murder.

16. Through sexual relations with non-Jews [lit. the nations] comes apostasy.

17. One who self appoints himself to a position of authority through this his daughter becomes a prostitute, GOD forbid.

18. Accountants, for the most part, are full of promiscuous lust.

19. One who does not look upon women merits that his descendants will compile commentaries on the Torah.

Foul language

1. Someone who speaks foul language, it is certain that in his heart he thinks thoughts of sin.

2. Through foul language comes adulation.

3. From the sin of foul language, troubles and evil decrees are renewed, and the young men of Israel die, GOD forbid, and orphans and widows cry out and are not answered.

4. One who defiles his speech, even if they have sealed for him a decree of seventy years for good, they reverse it to bad. Also, they deepen Hell for him. This also applies to one who hears [such speech] and remains silent.

5. More stringent is one who speaks verbally than the one who performs an action.

Sefer HaMidot

Test

1. A test is to bring greatness and fame to a man.

2. One who is not on the hierarchy of righteousness, and also does not have ancestral merit, and [nevertheless] wants to draw people to the service of the blessed GOD, he should guard himself from tests, and especially guard himself or so as, not to arouse the jealousy of the wicked.

3. One who is master over his desires, his children will not go off in bad ways, and through this his wealth is blessed, and through this, he will not come to be tested.

Falling

Part I

1. Sometimes, a man falls from his level in his old age.

2. Through collecting taxes, a man falls from his level.

3. Through jealousy one falls from his level.

4. Due to jealousy, a person does not have consistency. Sometimes he prays with enthusiasm and learns with diligence, and other times, the prayer and learning are a burden to him.

5. One who blunders in his speech [stammers - and certainly, one needs a fluent tongue for everything he needs to express - but one who [nevertheless] blunders in his speech, it is certain that his livelihood has been curtailed, and he is in need of great kindness and salvation, that the Holy One, Blessed be He, should grant him his livelihood.

6. By taking an oath, a person's longings can be recognized [alternate version: his longings are cut off. Both versions are

Sefer HaMidot

correct, however only one justifies this dictum to be categorized here under the entry of falling].

7. When a man slips and falls, this is because he had strengthened himself to commit a sin.

8. When you begin doing a mitzvah, and the beginning is with all your heart, you will be successful in fulfilling this mitzvah, and no harm will come to you.

9. One who falls from his awe of GOD, it is certain that his awe was not pure.

10. A person falls due to desire for money.

11. If you guard yourself from thievery, and from oaths, and from falsehood, you will not fall from your level.

12. When a man prays in a minyan which includes wicked people, they sometimes send him down. A segulah [to be protected] for this is to raise one's hands up during prayer.

13. One whose heart falls from its enthusiasm, it is because he hates the Tzaddik.

14. The Tzaddik who rules the world with Truth will not fall from his importance.

14. One who flees from honor and the honor pursues him, will certainly not descend from nor fall in prestige.

15. Through attachment to tzaddikim, one will not fall from one's level.

Part II
1. One who who is going [walking] and falls, should know that his guardian angels have deserted him.

Sefer HaMidot

2. One who has a thought of having relations with a gentile woman, it is certain that he will have some sort of fall.

3. Or some sickness will come upon his wife and children.

Memorial Lamp

1. In the merit of memorial [lit. constant] lamps that burn on olive oil, one is saved from losing the Jewish faith.

Auspicious Action or Object

1. Feathers from wild birds are a segulah for healing sicknesses of the lungs, and are conducive to strengthening the breath of life.

2. The heavens have changes in their appearance according to the appearance of the grasses that grow by them, and it is effective to gaze on them.

3. Rainwater [to drink] is a segulah for an impotent male.

4. Recital of Tehillim [Psalms] is a segulah for rainfall.

5. A segulah for renewing a woman's monthly cycle is to host guests.

6. Having hair that is unnaturally long is liable to causing much evil damage from the Other Side. A segulah against this is reciting the section [of the Torah reading] that is read on Yom Kippur.

7. Someone who becomes mute suddenly and unexpectedly, should pass a kosher butcher's knife over his mouth.

8. A segulah for a woman having difficulty giving birth is to

Sefer HaMidot

hang the key to the cemetery upon her neck.

9. It is a segulah for one suffering illness in the neck, to weep over the destruction of the Temple.

10. Upon entering a new house in which to live, it is a segulah to bring in a sword, knife or other weapon. An indication for this [from Scripture]: "Through wisdom a house is built" - the letters of "wisdom" [ChuChMah] stand for "Weapons of Violence they practice where they Reside". Their swords, their residence [the Hebrew word in the verse which was translated as "their residence" can be alternately translated: "their swords" [in which case the "weapons of violence" would be translated as, stolen weapons, see Rashi there]. [Thus, a connection between weapons and the maintaining of residence can be established].

11. Apples are a segulah for one who has difficulties in childbirth.

Secret

1. Through deep contemplation on the secrets of the Torah, one can bring conception to barren women and heal a serious illness.

The Counting of the Omer

1. Through counting of the omer, there is saving from expulsion.

2. Extra special care must be taken to dip [in a mikva] for one's accidental emission during the days of the omer.

3. In the counting of the omer it is possible to subdue an informer. A sign for this: "LaOMeR" [- to the omer - this is how the Omer is counted: 1 or 49 days to the Omer] this is

Sefer HaMidot

an acronym for: "Me'igra Rama L'bira Ohmika" [from a high roof to a deep pit].

Book

1. Someone who has the potential to write a book and does not; this is considered like losing children.

2. Writers must weigh the words of their books, to see if there is enough in them for a book. For the essence of a book is only the things which have been said with the connection of the souls, in the aspect of: "This is the book of the offspring of man." And if there is only a small amount from such a binding, then it is insufficient for a book.

3. When those with depth of understanding see novel Torah teachings in a book, they can discern whether the author conceived of them himself, or whether they were already existing beforehand from time immemorial one who conceived these novelties, and, because there had not been enough to comprise a book, these novelties were revealed to this author, for them to be included in his book, but in truth, he did not labor for these teachings, for they came to him with ease, for someone else had already toiled for them and brought them to revelation.

3. When some new Torah book is printed, the crying through which the book was created - in the aspect of "and my drink I mixed ["musachti" - close to "meseches" meaning tractate] with tears", this crying braces up against the decrees of the nations, that they should not overpower us. Furthermore, the main power of their sovereignty is only from the crying of Eisov. A sign of this: "And the number of the children of Israel will be as the sand of the sea."

4. One who does not look upon women, merits that his descendants will author commentaries on the Torah.

Sefer HaMidot

6. That which holy books by tzaddikim are buried [respectfully], and lost, and forgotten from the world, as with several books of the Tanaim and early Torah sages, which were lost and forgotten, this is beneficial for the world, for through this, many books by heretics and blasphemers, may their names be blotted out, are lost, uprooted and erased. Also, through this is annulled jealousy and hatred existing between an upright couple who live in holiness.

7. Through a significant book that comes into the world, barren women conceive. A hint for this: "This is the book of the offspring of man."

Redeeming Prisoners

Part I
1. Through haughtiness of the heart, one falls into incarceration.

2. One who agrees with the non-Jews falls into their hands. Rather, one should contradict all of their words.

3. Someone who says a statement in the name of the one who said it originator, brings redemption to the world.

4. Through redeeming prisoners, the redeemer's dispersed are gathered.

5. Someone who does not leave his house is considered as if incarcerated.

6. Through the sin of homosexuality, one becomes incarcerated the commentators do not provide any citation here, so I suggest a hint from Joseph who says - even here I did nothing to be deserving of incarceration - and we know from our Sages that Potephar, Joseph's master, had desired him and GOD had an angel castrate Potephar, so Joseph had

Sefer HaMidot

no cause whatsoever to have been incarcerated, so from here we can derive that homosexuality would be due cause.

7. Someone who has mercy on prisoners, the Holy One, Blessed be He, saves him from death.

8. Someone who is incarcerated, it is certain that his soul above is also incarcerated.

9. Someone who comes to the Tzadik and asks the Tzadik advice, and afterwards violates his advice, as a result, he becomes incarcerated.

10. One who feeds bread to the hungry, the Holy One, Blessed be He, saves him from the jailhouse.

11. One who did not fix the sins of his youth, as a result, he goes to the jail house.

12. Someone who is accustomed to performing circumcisions, or providing for the expenses of the circumcision feast for a poor person, through this, he is saved from the jail house [There is a hint to this from the Grace After Meals, who redeemed us from the house of bondage - through - your covenant that you sealed on our flesh - that is circumcision].

Part II
1. Through lewdness, one falls into incarceration or foot pain sickness. Also, a student who had not reached the level of delivering a halachic directive, yet prescribes, falls into this. Also, damaging spirits rule over or afflict him.

2. Charity is a segula [conductive] to nullifying all of those punishments.

3. Due to not requesting compassion on behalf of one's friend, as a result, one falls into incarceration. And a remedy

Sefer HaMidot

for incarceration is to support some living creature.

4. Through having marital relations on days on which such relations are forbidden, through this one falls into incarceration.

5. When one of the children of Israel falls into incarceration, as a result, according to his aspect, the wellsprings of wisdom are sealed up from the wise of the generation, and the opposite is true when he is freed from incarceration.

6. Sometimes, through incarceration, one is saved from loss of children.

7. Through lushon hura [slander], one becomes incarcerated.

8. The hairs that grow on a person and the clothes on a person at the time that he sits in captivity, an ugly spirit rests upon them which makes a person ugly and degraded.

9. Making an effort to free prisoners is a segula [conducive] for child-bearing.

10. Someone who is involved in freeing prisoners, through this, the great ones of the generation are included in him.

Codifiers of the Law

1. By learning the codes of Jewish law until one is able to render halachic decisions, one causes numerous barren women to conceive.

2. Through studying the Shulchan Aruch [the primary book of Jewish law], one comes to fear [of Heaven].

3. Learning Codes of Law annuls idolatrous thoughts.

4. When a wicked person rises in power, it becomes difficult to derive a new theory in the Codes. Also, the words of judges are not heard [acceptable] in the ears of the litigants.

Fear

Part I

1. At the time that an evildoer becomes afraid, it is certain that, at this time, the Holy One Blessed be He grants the Tzadik his desire.

2. Through fear comes stumbling.

3. Through trust in GOD, you will be saved from fear.

4. A segula [effective way] to nullify fear is to remember our father Avraham.

5. With charity, you will nullify fear.

6. An effective way to nullify fear is to say "Hashem Tzvaos".

7. Through fear, arrogance is nullified.

8. Fear saps a person's strength.

9. An intelligent person has nothing to fear from just a random noise.

10. Someone who becomes frightened, even though he does not see, his mazal [fortune] sees. To remedy this, he should jump from his place a distance of four cubits, or recite the Shema, or say, "the goats in the butcher shop are fatter than I".

Sefer HaMidot

11. Someone who has fears should sing a song of joy.

12. By picturing the name Elokim before your eyes, fears will leave you.

13. Someone who consumes Jewish money, fears come to him.

14. Someone who is not careful with the blessings at the beginning and end [of eating], fears come to him.

15. Through trust in GOD, you will not have fear.

16. Willow branches beaten [on Hoshana Rabba] have segula [are conducive] to nullifying fear.

17. One who listens to and obeys a Torah courts decision Torah law, will be saved from fear.

18. Three hundred and ten immersions [in a mikva- ritual bath] nullify fear. One should also give a gift to a Tzadik.

19. Through truth, a person is saved from fear at night.

20. Through humility, you will not have fear.

21. A house in which there is fear, it is certain that the Other Side has a portion in it.

22. When there is some fear and, afterwards, a fire – burnin comes, it is certain that the fear will be annulled.

23. Fear comes through adulation.

24. When Israel is united, the nations fear them.

25. When they forget Hashem, may He be Blessed, and do not rely on him, through this, they fear the nations.

Sefer HaMidot

26. Through worry comes fear.

27. Through fear comes lies.

28. The light of a candle is a segula for [conducive to reducing] fear.

29. Through boasting of wealth comes fear.

30. Fear comes through anger.

31. Through worry and fear, the heart becomes sealed [insensitive].

32. By learning Torah at the table at mealtime, one is saved from fear.

33. Someone who has fear - this is a sign that the Holy One, Blessed be He, hides His Face from him, and a sign that judgments rest on him.

34. One who does not confess his sins - fear comes to him.

Part II
1. When fear comes to a person, he should know that someone who shares his mazal has come into some trouble.

2. Sometimes a person becomes afraid before some good comes to him.

3. Someone who flees from trouble is smart.

4. On a night that you have fear when it is time to sleep, do not go on the road in the day.

5. When a person is on the verge of death, even if he is still healthy and does not know of his death sentence, nonetheless, he becomes afraid and says verbally that he will die.

Sefer HaMidot

Abstinence

1. One who conducts himself with abstinence and afterwards retracts from it, falls into additional craving, more than he had before his abstention.

2. Abstinence brings satiety.

3. Abstinence from sexual relations is reckoned as a fast.

4. The sickness of coughing up blood is due to canceling [or refraining from] sexual relations of the night of one's wife's ritual immersion.

Sin

1. There are sins that the place or location instigates.

2. Someone who commits a sin in order to anger GOD, not for self gratification: In the end, he will be derided in the eyes of others, and he will be enraged at them.

Punishment

1. Sometimes, when a person performs a mitzva Divine commandment or good deed and the Holy One, Blessed be He, punishes him, this is because he did not perform a similar Divine commandment when he had the opportunity to do so.

2. Sometimes a person is judged according to his own words [Generally Jewish Law does not give veracity to self implication].

3. Sometimes a man is murdered because he had the ability to advocate on behalf of someone who was being hated for no reason.

Sefer HaMidot

4. Sometimes a man is punished because of negligence in his work, or because a decree had been passed upon the people of his community or upon his nation.

5. The Holy One, Blessed be He, is swift to punish those who are ungrateful through the agency of those who are ungrateful.

6. Someone who was bit by a dog, it is certain that he accepted slander [lushon hura] or spoke slander.

Brazenness

Part I

1. One who is brazen, it is certain that he has transgressed out of spite.

2. Brazenness comes through anger.

3. Through brazenness, one will not accept mussar [ethical criticism].

4. Through brazenness, one's heart becomes armored and it is also certain that he has yet to repair the sins of his father.

5. One who is brazen, his rectification is to don tefillin [phylacteries] that had been on the head of a tzaddik.

6. When an evildoer acts brazenly before an upright man, this is only so that the upright one will examine his deeds.

7. One who is brazen, assuredly he is not making do with what he has.

8. The Torah is a rectification for brazenness.

9. Through brazenness, rains are withheld. And it is certain that he stumbled in a sin and, in the end, will stumble in more sin. It is permitted to call him "wicked", and it is permitted to hate him, and he is from one of the 974 generations.

10. Audacity, even against Heaven, is effective, but it is considered as ruling without a crown [that is illegitimately].

Part II
1. When one sees everyone brazen to the faces of the Torah scholars, it is certain that great wars will be aroused against this nation.

2. Headaches come upon one who is brazen to the face of someone from the seed of King David.

Humility

Part I
1. One who shares in the suffering of the Jewish People, and prays for them, through this he comes to humility.

2. Through truth, one will merit to humility.

3. Through faith one comes to submission.

4. Through retaining a specific place for prayer, one comes to humility and piety [hassidut].

5. Through humility one's prayer is heard, and it is as if he had offered all the sacrifices.

6. Through humility, additional greatness is added to one's greatness.

7. Through humility, one's days are lengthened.

8. Through humility, one's deeds are not scrutinized.

Sefer HaMidot

9. The day on which you humble yourself, that day adds strength, might and exaltation to the Holiness Above.

10. When you see that humility is increasing in the world, be expectant for the footsteps of the Messiah.

11. Through humility, fear of enemies is annulled.

12. Through humility, contention and suffering is annulled.

13. Through [one's having] humility, everyone is at peace with him.

14. Through humility comes grace.

15. One who has the quality of submission, does not have fear, as if he were sitting in a fortress.

16. Someone without the quality of submission has no fear [of Heaven].

17. Through humility one becomes great, also he does not fall from his level.

18. Someone who is soft hearted, he can submit himself more extremely or to the extreme.

19. Through humility, the Holy One Blessed is He remembers one.

20. Through humility, the Holy One Blessed is He fulfills one's desires.

21. The world is only sustained by one who makes himself as nothing.

Part II
A segulah [auspicious] for having sons is to humble oneself.

Sefer HaMidot

2. Through excessive arrogance, one will be sodomized like a woman.

3. One can recognize in a man's voice, whether he is humble or Arrogant.

4. Sometimes, through the lowliness with which a person diminishes himself, or through others diminishing him, through this is annulled a decree of death which was passed upon him.

5. When a person senses lowliness in himself, he should know that death has been decreed upon him.

Depression

Part I

1. One who has not rectified the sins of his youth, through this worries come upon him.

2. For the most part, suffering comes to a man through his speech.

3. When you are suffering, speak about this suffering.

4. Through worries of the heart, falls upon the person fear of death.

5. Through submission, evil and sorrow are annulled.

6. One who is depressed should gaze upon the tzaddikim, and joy will come to his heart.

7. When you enter the house of a non-Jew, through this depression comes upon you.

8. Through depression one becomes weakened.

Sefer HaMidot

9. Through an evil heart, one's face is transformed.

10. When you have anguish on a day of joy, and all your happiness is dispelled, know that your ancestral merit has been exhausted.

11. One who is depressed should continually give a gift to a tzaddik.

12. Through depression come fires burnings.

13. Depression is a sign that some disease is about to manifest.

14. Due to depression, the Holy One, Blessed be He, is not with him.

15. Through depression, one has [lit. sees] a wasteful unintentional seminal emission.

16. Depression comes through anger.

17. Through depression, a person does not reach his aspiration.

18. Due to depression, one is degraded.

19. Due to weeping, a person is unable to eat.

20. One who is not depressed, but is always joyful, will certainly be raised up.

21. Through depression comes degradation.

22. Crying is a positive sign for a sick person.

23. Through anguish, one's enemies are highly elevated.

Sefer HaMidot

24. Through anguish comes heart pain.

25. One who is hasty is gloomy sad and annoyed and irritated.

26. Drawing close to tzaddik im makes the heart joyous.

27. A segulah for removing depression is to listen to an honored tzaddik when he sings.

28. One who does not confess his sins has sighing and worries come upon him.

29. When a person lusts after things that are against [the Will of] the Holy One, Blessed be He, through this anguish [sighing] comes upon him.

30. Sadness due to a bad dream annuls the influence of the dream, preventing it from coming to pass.

31. Voice, appearance, and scent restore a person's wellbeing [lit. knowledge or awareness].

32. Through screaming, one's pain is annulled.

33. One who is depressed brings suffering upon himself.

34. One who draws too far after his own suffering, suffering draws towards him.

35. Dates annul worry.

36. Aggadah [Talmudic legends] brings joy to a man.

Part II
1. Depression fills the heart of a man when he becomes aware of his own evil and bad fortune. For the heart causes all of this, because the heart

is the cause of everything; for good or for bad [lit. the opposite].

2. One must guard himself from depression in order that he not come to mourning, GOD forbid.

3. Through suffering and sadness, conflict comes into the world. Conversely, through joy, peace comes to the world.

4. Through the spoiling of one's joy, sicknesses come upon him.

5. It is a segulah to remove depression through mercy.

6. Vows and pledges bring happiness.

Advice

1. Do not ask advice except from one who knows secrets of the Torah.

2. It is good to ask advice from the elderly.

3. One who gives his fellow advice inappropriate for him, through this he is beset by idolatrous thoughts.

4. Someone who is accustomed to having bad thoughts, do not take advice from him.

5. Through that which you take advice from the official rabbi, through this you will merit salvation.

6. When you see that your friends are not helping you, it is known that no advice or remedy will help you.

7. When you help the Jewish People, advice can help you.

Sefer HaMidot

8. Advice is more auspicious [segula] in a field.

9. One who follows the advice of his wife falls into Hell.

10. Do not ask advice; only from a man, and not from a woman.

Constipation

1. Through constipation come idolatrous thoughts.

2. In any case of impending death, one should open his orifices.

3. Constipation harms the eyes.

Laziness

1. Through the desires that a man desires, but does not attain them, through this comes laziness. This is also the case in the converse.

2. Through zeal, one removes sleep and enlivens the mind.

Righteous

Part I
1. It should not be difficult to you when you see that a tzaddik did not repair something, for this was intended by GOD, that he, the tzadik should leave something for his children to repair and thereby become great with it.

2. There are times when neglecting the study of Torah is its foundation.

Sefer HaMidot

3. Gifts are permitted to be accepted from the wicked, so that they should return in repentance.

4. Tzaddikim, their merit is beneficial for the world, but not for themselves.

5. There are cases in which one tzaddik does something, in order to be the rabbi of another tzaddik.

6. It is very beneficial to see the faces of the leaders [lit. great] of the generation.

7. A tzaddik is punished when he does not pray for his generation.

8. One who teaches Torah to a student who is not becoming, is called "wicked".

9. The language of the sages brings wealth and healing. This being the case, learn to speak in their language [Language here is referring to word choice, phraseology, and maxims].

10. One who teaches Torah to others, the Torah is revealed to him without effort.

11. We find that a tzaddik becomes belligerent when one of his students draws himself close to another tzaddik in order to glorify himself.

12. Drawing close to tzaddikim with strenuous effort is more supportive to serving GOD [More than making the same achievement without the effort].

13. Sometimes, from Heaven there is revealed to a tzaddik, something with is not.

14. One who does a favor for someone who is not aware of it, is as one who throws a stone to Marculis [an ancient form of idolatry].

15. Every man should conduct himself according to what he heard from his rabbi.

16. Sometimes GOD gathers several tzaddikim together in one place, so that they will press upon each other and be discomfited, and through this, they will come to their maturity.

17. One who does not hold back from relieving himself, merits to students.

18. There is a tzaddik whose repute travels far, that is to say, with fame, and afterwards he falls through desiring money.

19. One who the Holy One Blessed He is important in his eyes, should write in a book all the names of the tzaddikim, and the tannaim [the rabbis who compiled the Mishnah], and the GOD fearing, for remembrance.

20. Do not question why do the tzaddikim benefit from others in order to conduct their households with wealth and honor - Would it not be better for them to not conduct - and not benefit from others, do not have this difficulty. Because for all the delight and expansion the Tzaddik has, his soul grows greater, and then there is created a House of Rest or Prophecy- that is a Temple] for the Divine Presence of the Holy One Blessed He. Thus, one should not come to the house of the Tzaddik empty-handed.

21. When you want a tzaddik to pray for you, go to a tzaddik who is merciful.

22. One who is famous in his generation, you should call him "Rabbi", even if you greater than him.

23. When a tzaddik falls into some crisis, he should ask another tzaddik to pray on his behalf.

24. Those people who travel to a tzaddik, even if they do not receive a Torah teaching from him, they are rewarded for the journey.

25. One who does not serve Torah scholars is liable to the death penalty.

26. The tzaddik can bring departed souls up to a great level.

27. In the walking that one does to come to a Torah scholar, with this he rectifies an infraction that he violated in the blessings of 'neh-henin' [benefit, pleasure; these are blessings said before eating or smelling a fragrance].

28. Anyone who is capable of protesting and did not protest, is punished on their account.

29. It is not courteous to acknowledge the authority of others in front of the Tzaddik.

30. All who are lethargic with the eulogy of a Torah scholar will not have length of years.

31. The Tzaddik can punish according to his fortune.

32. When a tzaddik passes away, the world is world is met out a deficiency according to his distinguishing attribute that he conducted.

33. In the merit of the Tzaddik, his students attain their livelihood.

34. One who hears a Torah teaching from the Tzaddik is as if he himself said the teaching.

35. The death of tzaddikim is as grave as the burning of the

Temple [lit. the House of our GOD].

36. If a Torah scholar is an upright person, learn from him, and if not, separate yourself from him.

37. One should not look upon his rabbi in the bathhouse and the like.

38. Sometimes there are two equal tzaddikim, and to one there is revealed lofty things, while the other has no revelations. Know that this that he is not shown anything is because it is necessary to use his merits for the protection of others.

39. It is better to draw close to a tzaddik who is merciful.

40. In the merit of serving a great man, one is saved from death.

41. One who rules a halachic [Jewish law] decision in the presence of his rabbi is liable to the death penalty, and it is fitting for a snake to bite him, and he is called a sinner, and he is cast down from his greatness, and he descends to Hell childless.

42. The source from which one draws wisdom - that is, the Rabbi - be sure that he is blessed and worthy, and do not replace him and do not exchange him.

33. Every Jew should or will conduct himself in accordance with the blessing that was given to his tribe.

34. When there is an evildoer in the house, the wellsprings of the Torah depart from the Tzaddik.

35. In the merit of the tzaddikim buried outside of Israel, the other corpses will also merit to be transported to Israel through rolling in underground passages.

Sefer HaMidot

46. The money from which a tzaddik benefits is as if it had been used for the service in the Holy Temple.

47. There are tzaddikim who are not called by the title of Rebbe.

48. When a tzaddik says something, as long as it does not come to pass, because its time has not come, the statement is engraved in the supernal world, but does not radiate brightly, and when its time comes to be manifest, the words begin to radiate brightly.

49. One who gives benefit to a Torah scholar must strengthen himself, that the scholar should not become disrespected in his eyes.

50. One who withholds a halacha [Torah law] from his student is as if he stole the student's ancestral inheritance. Even fetuses in their mothers' wombs curse him and pierce him full of holes as a sieve. If he teaches him or it - the student or the halacha], he merits to blessings like Joseph, and merits to teach it also in the World to Come, In the Talmud this last point is a new one, objective of the halacha, not subjective to a student.

51. One who does not give support to a Torah scholar from his possessions will never see a sign of blessing.

52. One who scoffs at the words of the sages is punished by death.

53. Drawing close to tzaddikim is beneficial both in this world and the next world.

54. The Tzaddik, through his word, can sentence one man to Heaven and another to Hell.

55. It is good to expend much time in order to gain one hour of closeness to the Tzaddik.

56. When a man loses some of his servants, he should worry from the day of death, or of something else.

57. There is one who expounds beautifully on the Torah, and even still be miss the true intention.

58. A tzaddik can raise up the Torah teaching of another tzaddik.

59. Whatever new teachings a tzaddik propounds in the Torah, the Holy One Blessed He quotes them in his name.

60. The words of wise tzaddikim are more precious than the words of the written Torah and the Prophets. One must listen and obey them, even if they show no proof.

61. One who praises the Tzaddik, blessings will rest upon his head.

62. The Tzaddik of a city - all of its affairs are incumbent upon him.

63. It is permitted for a tzaddik to put to his service someone who reviews halachah, that is a Torah scholar, provided that he the tzadik teaches him, the attendant something new.

64. One who brings a boorish or uneducated man to be drawn close under the wings of the Tzaddik, receives reward for it.

65. Through greeting a Torah authority, one will not see Hell.

66. Sometimes, prayer is only effective at the time it is said, and when the prayer is stopped, the Holy One Blessed He returns and does His will and His desire.

Sefer HaMidot

67. One who brings a gift to a Torah scholar is as if he offered Bikurim [offering of the first fruit].

68. One should not unduly task GOD [lit. The Place - for GOD is the place of the world].

69. One who loves the Tzaddik must guard the Tzaddik, so that there doesn't go out on him a bad reputation.

70. All the good and the kindness that wicked people, do is harmful bad to the tzaddikim.

71. Do not pray and burden your Creator, so long as you can reach your objective through your own action.

72. The tzaddik as long as he is in this world, the Heaven [gan eden] that is reserved for him is used by other tzaddikim in Heaven.

73. There are students who are primarily dependent on the merit of the Tzaddik. When the tzaddik passes away, then they too pass away, or they are punished.

74. Those who are close to a certain tzaddik in his lifetime, they will be close to him after his death [there is an alternate reading - their death].

75. One who had been close to one tzaddik, and afterwards draws close to a different tzaddik, the Torah teachings he heard from the first encumber him.

76. Sometimes a tzaddik passes away, in order to be the pivotal decider of some ruling Above.

77. Who is destined to inherit the World to Come? One who is granted honor due to his wisdom.

78. Through giving charity, one gains the quality of

Sefer HaMidot

distancing himself from wrongdoing.

79. It is not necessary to punish your student and banish him from your presence, when he does not want to go in the straight path. Rather, draw him close to you, for this is beneficial to the other students, and eventually he will reform [lit. give heart].

80. Sometimes a man dies before his time due to the grievance of a tzaddik against him.

81. It is possible for a man to be a great tzaddik, even though he did not learn a lot.

82. One who does not believe in the words of the tzaddikim is fit to be punished, all the more so one who ridicules them.

83. When one comes to draw close to a tzaddik, he the tzaddik, is allowed to distance him when he asks unnecessary questions.

84. When a tzaddik delivers a Torah teaching to the people, he is permitted to endear his teaching in their eyes before he says it.

85. Even a person's first intended soulmate can be changed through prayer.

86. In this world anyone who wants to bring himself close - can draw close. But in the World to Come, only those who were already close will be drawn closer.

87. A tzaddik who drew a person close, but the person did not want to draw himself close, it is permitted for him, the tzaddik, to push him away with his hands.

88. The Tzaddik can punish a person with death, even through being disheartened - even mistakenly.

Sefer HaMidot

89. Things that you hear directly from the mouth of a tzaddik are more effective than what you learn from books.

90. A person understands better when he sees the face of the speaker.

91. Through the casual [lit. light] speech of the Tzaddik, a great light is opened up. Then it is easy for people to attain high wisdoms.

92. One who does not behave properly, it is permitted to enslave him.

93. Sometimes a tzaddik raises up a man, and then humbles him, and this is for the man's benefit.

94. There is a tzaddik who is called "good", and there is a tzaddik who is not called "good", and there is an evildoer who is evil, and an evildoer who is not evil.

95. It is a disgrace, and lowliness of the generation, when the people are subject to a leader who has no one to do his work for him.

96. To teach others Torah is greater than doing, actual fulfillment of the Torah.

97. One should be careful not to show hasidus, special piety in keeping the Torah and devotion to GOD, before great people or leaders.

98. The essence of a man is recognizable according to his drawing close, by seeing to whom he his close.

99. A tzaddik should not endanger himself by praying alone, to the extent that he is endangered, rather he should have another tzaddik join him.

Sefer HaMidot

100. A tzaddik has the power to pray for a man, that he should be saved from sins.

101. The Tzaddik is the image of GOD [that man was created in.] of the generation.

102. The Tzaddik bears those who bear him at the time of their pain.

103. It is possible for someone to be a tzaddik, even if he does not possess the trait of trust in GOD in completeness.

104. The Tzaddik can take delight, from the physical world, and need not fear from the evil inclination, for his Torah protects him.

105. Someone who does not stand up before his rabbi is called "wicked", and does not live a long life, and his Torah learning is forgotten.

106. One should not burden the blessed GOD, when one can be helped through other means.

107. Sometimes, through one bit of satisfaction one brings to the Tzaddik, through this one merits to the World to Come.

108. One who has complete faith in the blessed GOD can give satisfaction to the Tzaddik.

109. One who does not have a trace of thoughts of idolatry, he constantly longs to save the tzaddikim.

110. One who wants to do a favor for the Tzaddik, the Holy One Blessed He gives him strength for it.

111. A Torah scholar who shows impudence to his rabbis causes his years to be shortened.

Sefer HaMidot

112. One who conducts himself with Rabbinic authority when there is someone greater than him, his years are shortened.

113. When a tzaddik needs to pray to be given something, and he fears from forces challenging his righteousness, he should ask for the opposite of what he wants.

114. When a wicked man does some evil, and comes to the Tzaddik and asks him if what he [the wicked mad] did was acceptable, it is permissible for the Tzaddik to tell him, "You did well", in order to save himself [lit. his soul].

115. One who separates people from coming under the wings of the Divine Presence causes his sons to fall into slavery.

116. Sometimes it is necessary to pray for mercy on a sick person - that he should die.

117. First the Holy One Blessed He reveals a secret of the Torah to a tzaddik, and afterwards, the Holy One Blessed He says this Torah in the name of that tzaddik.

118. Sometimes the tzaddik fasts and prays, and it does not help.

119. It is permitted for the Tzaddik to break through the [religious] safeguards of others to forge his own way.

120. Sometimes it is decreed from Above that a number of people should die, and there is one among them that the Tzaddik loves. The Tzaddik has the power to pray for him, and save him, and put another in his place.

121. A tzaddik has the power to take from one and give to another.

122. The blessing of a tzaddik is a pidyon, redemption,

ransom.

123. Each tzaddik has a matter of devotion that another tzaddik, even one greater than he, cannot attain conception of his service.

124. That which tzaddikim travel from place to place for to raise money, it is because the words of Torah are poor in one place and rich in another, this saying is usually intended to describe the process of learning something from one passage in the Torah, and applying it to a different passage.

125. Length of years comes to Torah scholars when they honor each other.

126. There is no comparing the prayer of a tzaddik who is the son of a tzaddik, to the prayer of a tzaddik who is the son of a wicked man.

127. One who puts the Tzaddik to the test is as if he tests the Holy One Blessed He.

128. All the levies that the nations demand from the Jewish People are only due to their have violated the honor of the Tzaddik.

129. When those who hate GOD slander and stand against the Tzaddik, it is a great honor for the Tzaddik.

130. Through faith in tzaddikim, the din [judgement] is sweetened.

131. The Tzaddik teaches GOD through his Torah [exegesis], how to deal with us.

132. The prayer a person prays with attachment to the tzaddikim, it is answered.

Sefer HaMidot

133. The Holy One Blessed He forgives the sins of Israel for the sake of the tzaddikim.

134. The mockery [inside a person, or his fear of being mocked, or both], does not allow one to go to the tzaddikim.

135. Through charity, one merits to come close to tzaddikim.

136. There is no tzaddik who does not have a conflict on him and investigators.

137. There is a type of evildoer who is ashamed to blaspheme the Tzaddik himself, and so he slanders those that are under the Tzaddik.

138. Through seeing the face of the Tzaddik, the intellect is sharpened.

140. One who protects the Tzaddik, that no suffering should come to him, will merit to honor, and will benefit from the righteousness of the Tzaddik.

141. Through hearing Torah directly from the [mouth of the] Tzaddik, one receives vitality.

142. An evildoer who has committed many sins, his rectification is - that his actions should be [geared] to give vitality to the Tzaddik.

143. When an evildoer submits himself under the Tzaddik, it is certain that some hardship had been decreed upon the Tzaddik, and now the hardship will no longer come upon him.

144. When you have fear of the tzaddik, you will merit to distance yourself from wrongdoing.

145. When a tzaddik is set with pain, and an evildoer asks for mercy on his behalf, through this he will merit in the future to stand at the gates of a tzaddik.

146. That which the Holy One Blessed He does not heed the prayer of the tzaddik, it is in order to thus reject the evildoers, that they should remain in their wickedness.

147. Through conflict on the Tzaddik, the Torah is forgotten.

148. The praise that is extolled of the tzaddikim is as if it is praise to the Holy One Blessed He.

149. A city that obeys the Tzaddik, no war is heard in it, and there are no upheavals or evil tidings.

150. The opposition to the tzaddikim comes from the opposition between the tzaddikim themselves.

151. For this reason, the Holy One Blessed He gives livelihood to a tzaddik through the general populace, in order that he will have some connection with them, and so that when the Holy One Blessed He remembers the tzaddik, He will remember them as well.

152. The coming of the Messiah depends on drawing close to the Tzaddik.

153. The primary fulfillment of the soul comes through drawing close to the tzaddikim.

154. Someone who draws close to the Tzaddik, but his drawing close is not with sincerity or innocence, through this he is turned around afterwards to be an opposer.

155. A liar - when he comes to see the Tzaddik - his heart contemplates how he will speak afterwards.

155. The words that people speak against the Tzaddik, in the end their words are turned around against them, and they fall bedridden.

156. One who submits himself before the Tzaddik, with this he arouses the love of the Tzaddik.

157. Through the stories of the tzaddikim, through this one merits to draw close to them.

158. According to the Divine Inspiration the Holy One Blessed He grants to a tzaddik, so the wealthy people support him. According to the support they give him, so he can bring the evildoers back in repentance.

159. The suffering that comes upon the tzaddikim, is so that in the World to Come, the wicked will not question in their minds the good that the Holy One Blessed He will be giving the tzaddikim.

160. When the GOD fearing is connected to the Tzaddik, through this they cause a union between the Holy One, Blessed be He, and the Divine Presence, face to face, and there is no regression from this afterwards.

161. Through the praises that one extolls the tzaddikim, the wicked are pushed down to a great fall.

162. The Tzaddik passes away due to the sins of witchcraft and promiscuity.

163. The promiscuous are for the most part opposers of the tzaddikim.

164. When the Tzaddik passes away, the world, the people remain as though impure, and the righteousness of the world is disgusting in the eyes of the Holy One Blessed He.

Sefer HaMidot

165. Through the haughtiness people hold above the Tzaddik, there is aroused, GOD forbid, Divine wrath. Also fires [lit. burning] are aroused.

166. The wandering about of the tzaddikim is sometimes in order to reveal some hidden tzaddik.

167. Sometimes suffering comes upon the Tzaddik, in order to decrease the hardships of Israel.

168. The gluttonous eating [lit. the filling of the stomach, which does not have to denote gluttony but eating very well] of the masses causes the loss of the Tzaddik.

169. The sufferings that come upon the tzaddikim are an atonement for all of the Jewish People.

170. One who does not want to accept upon himself the yoke of the Tzaddik, the Holy One Blessed He is angry at him and kicks him.

171. One who brings a gift to the Tzaddik, the Holy One Blessed He gives him satisfaction.

172. Through the gifts that people bring to tzaddikim, the enemies are subdued, and there is annulment of the evil spirit that sets upon a person.

173. Through prostrating oneself on the tombs of tzaddikim, the Holy One Blessed He does favors for him, even if he is not worthy of such.

174. Someone who recounts stories of the tzaddikim, the Holy One Blessed He does him kindness.

175. That which the Tzaddik rules over the world people is due to the fear of GOD within him.

Sefer HaMidot

176. When a man is being blessed by the Tzaddik, he should stand on his feet.

177. A king is permitted to levy his expenses from the people.

178. Through the honor people extend to the children of the tzaddikim, the desire is aroused in the blessed GOD for the arrival of the Messiah

179. Through the act of going - that people go to the Tzaddik, they subdue the wicked.

180. One who transgresses the command of the Tzaddik, he falls from his importance.

181. One who gives the Tzaddik enjoyment or benefit from his property, is as if he benefited all of Israel, and he is saved from death.

182. One who disobeys by refusal to perform the words of the Tzaddik is as if he engaged in the asking of sorcerers.

183. Through wisdom, GOD is with one, and also the fear of him is cast upon the people.

184. One who supports the Tzaddik with all types of support, he is close and near to him in the World to Come.

185. One who starts up with the Tzaddik, in the end he is caught in a bad trap.

186. One who recounts the stories of tzaddikim, his righteousness is recalled.

187. The Tzaddik can give something that has not yet come into the world.

188. The Tzaddik - everywhere his feet tread, he acquires.

Sefer HaMidot

189. Someone who gives advice to tzaddikim at a time when they are facing opposition, the work of his hands endures, and will not be annulled.

190. At the time when one looks upon the Tzaddik, he should look with dread, so that he will not be punished by Heaven.

191. Through fear of Heaven, a person gains a longing to draw himself close to the Tzaddik.

192. Through sitting at the table of the Tzaddik, war is annulled.

193. One who is a forger, in the end he will join the opposers who stand against the Tzaddik.

194. Sometimes the plague of leprosy breaks out upon the Tzaddik, because he had recently brought someone back in repentance.

195. Someone who says of a tzaddik that he is wicked, and of a wicked one that he is a tzaddik, through this he falls into a state of weakness, also the sun and moon are eclipsed.

196. Connection to the Tzaddik is a great healing.

197. It is hard for a man to receive a salvation, when there is a tzaddik in the city, and he the man does not ask the tzaddik to pray for him.

198. Sometimes a person comes very close to the Tzaddik, and yet does not feel within himself any fear of Heaven. He should know that if he had not come close, he would not be worthy of living at all.

199. Sometimes a tzaddik is ashamed to pray to the Holy One Blessed He about his personal suffering. What does the Holy One Blessed He do? He brings similar suffering upon an evildoer, so that when the evildoer comes and asks from him the tzaddik to pray for him, and through this, the tzaddik is also saved from his suffering

200. One who disputes the Tzaddik in front of him, it is certain that he does not have fear of Heaven.

201. Sometimes the controversy surrounding a tzaddik is a great proof that he is a tzaddik.

202. There is an evildoer who is successful. But when he pursues or attacks, the Tzaddik, the klipos, husks - impure forces, themselves take revenge on him.

203. The difference between a tzaddik and one who has fear of Heaven, is that the one with fear does not have permission to reveal the mysteries of the Holy One Blessed He, whereas the tzaddik has permission.

204. One who slanders the Tzaddik, it is certain that he is arrogant.

205. When the Holy One Blessed He wants the Tzaddik to teach the people the Way of GOD, He hints this to him through his livelihood.

206. The Tzaddik - when he prays on behalf of someone, he can discern from which sin this suffering came upon the person.
207. Someone who guards his covenant, sexual purity, will certainly have love for the Tzaddik.

206. When the Tzaddik serves the blessed GOD, without supervising the masses to teach them, through this he falls from his level.

Through the income people provide for the livelihood of the Tzaddik, all their sins are forgiven. Just as we find in the

Torah the Cohanim priests eat of the sacrifices and by this the owners those that brought the sacrifices are atoned.

Part II

1. Through the stories of tzaddikim, one draws the light of Messiah into the world, and pushes out much darkness and hardship from the world.

2. Also, one merits to nice clothing.

3. In the seven days of mourning over the Tzaddik, the Holy One Blessed He dispenses on the mourners from the hidden light of the Six Days of Creation.

4. Do not be puzzled on the scheme, that man is a small creature and all the worlds are contingent on him. For such is the way with every place wherein the Divine Presence pervades; the little holds the great and many.

5. Every man has drawn in his visage his portion in gan eden [Heaven].

6. For the most part, the GOD fearing - their livelihood comes through moving about.

7. Sometimes the Tzaddik comes to moving from place to place, so that when he comes to the World to Come, he will remember all the places he had been, and through this good will come to all those places.

8. Someone who knows the names of the children of the tzaddikim of the generation, he knows all the events that are yet to come.

9. Someone who justifies the people, all his interests are fulfilled without hindrance.

10. When a tzaddik's strength is weakened, so that he cannot do the will of his Creator as before, he should know that the Holy One Blessed He no longer desires that he instruct the way of repentance to the wicked.

11. **The** main strength of the tzaddikim comes when the judgment is sweetened, that is, through the unification of the blessed name of GOD.

12. **When** the tzaddikim become famous in the world, through this there are new melodies in the world.

13. **One** who has self-sacrifice for the sake Israel, the judgments he passes are not annulled, and what he decrees will be fulfilled.

14. **Through** serving the Tzaddik comes freedom, and the curses are annulled.

15. **Those** who are close to GOD fearing, they also merit fear and cognizance.

16. **When** a tzaddik becomes wealthy, through this the wicked return in repentance.

17. **When** the Holy One Blessed He sees that a certain tzaddik has the power to draw people to His service, He stands up on him enemies, in order that he will be able to draw the people to GOD. Because a tzaddik who does not have enemies, he cannot draw people to GOD. This is comparable to the time of the arrival of the Messiah, they will reside in peace, and then converts will not be accepted.

18. **There** are two tzaddikim, that one, his words are like plowing, and the second, his words are like harvesting. Or one, his words are like the erection of the covenant [male member] for conjugation, and the second, his words are what draws the seed to impregnation and form the fetus in its mother's womb and develop it. Thus, when there is an

Sefer HaMidot

argument between these two tzaddikim, an outsider should not interfere in their words which they say against each other, so that he does not ruin the intended aim.

19. When one goes to the tombs of the tzaddikim, one needs merit to be able to draw his the tzaddik's spirit and soul, to the tomb, so it will be, as if he is alive. For if there isn't merit, then his the tzaddik's, spirit and soul ascend to Heaven, to the midst of the other tzaddikim.

20. Through mentioning the names of the tzaddikim, one can bring changes in the Creation, that is to say, to change nature do the supernatural. An indication for this matter is: "These arethe offspring or chronicles of the Heaven and the Earth", and "These arethe names of the children of Israel" - syllogism.

21. One who knows from the Land of Israel, who has truly tasted the taste of the Land of Israel, he can recognize in another if he had been by a tzaddik on Rosh Ha Shana [the Jewish New Years] or not. Because one who merits to be by a true tzaddik on Rosh ha Shana, then in every place where this person looks, the air of that place becomes the aspect of the air of the Land of Israel. Therefore, one who knows from the taste of the Land of Israel, each according to his level, it is imperative for him to sense the Land of Israel, when he meets and gets together with this man who had been by the true tzaddik on Rosh Ha Shana. For at his hand the air becomes of the aspect of the Land of Israel, as explained above.

Charity

Part I
1. All the charity and kindness that the Jewish People do in this world engenders great peace and [the formation of] angelic advocates between Israel and their Father in Heaven.

Sefer HaMidot

2. Great is charity, in that it brings the Redemption near.

3. And saves from death.

4. And causes the receiving of the Divine Presence.

5. And one is made a lender to the Holy Blessed One.

6. And raises his fortune [mazal].

7. And he is called a tzaddik completely, that is an absolutely righteous person.

8. Through charity, a person becomes [a fulfillment of Biblical injuction] "avoid evil".

9. It is a greater mitzva [good Torah deed] to provide food for those who study [literally - occupied with] the Torah than for those who do not study. However, from the standpoint of halachah [religious law], there is no grounds to differentiate.

10. When one extracts stolen goods from the hands of his fellowman, it is as if he has given charity.

11. Compromise is a legal judgment wherein there is charity, translators note: that part which is forfeited to the other litigant.

12. One who gives charity to an improper poor person is not rewarded for it.

13. It is necessary to be appreciative to one who gives, and you should not say that he didn't give of his own.

14. Charity has the importance of all the other commandments combined.

15. The one who brings another to do [that is give charity,

Sefer HaMidot

that is the one collecting the charity] is greater than the one who does, who gives the charity.

16. Every penny and penny of charity one gives is added together into a large sum.

17. One who gives charity in a hidden manner is greater than Moshe [Moses]. translators note: This has to be understood in context of the regular function of Moshe as the leader of Israel, because obviously Moshe also gave charity in a hidden manner.

18. One who gives a coin to a poor person is blessed with six blessings, and one who placates him is blessed with eleven blessings.

19. One who pursues opportunities to give charity, GOD provides him with money, and provides him with upright people in need of charity, in order that he should gain reward from giving charity to them, and he merits having children who are wealthy, wise, and masters of Aggadah

20. On Rosh HaShana, man is judged how much money he will lose, that is fail to keep. If he merits, he gives that money to the poor.

21. Jerusalem is redeemed with charity.

22. Through charity, Achav - one of the evillest Kings of Israel, was forgiven half of his sins.

23. Hospitality protects one from the, punishment of the sin of idolatry.

24. Great is hospitality, in that makes those who are close to holiness distanced. tranlator's note: If the purpose of the hospitality was to bring the guest to sin, and brings near to holiness those who are distant.

Sefer HaMidot

25. One who invites a non-Jew into his house and serves him causes his children to be exiled.

26. When the people do not give charity, the government passes harsh decrees and takes their money.

27. One should give charity with both hands which causes his prayer to be heard.

28. Through generosity you will have a standing.

29. Through charity comes faith.

30. One who goes out for the benefit of charities, sedates rage from the world.

31. Also, he merits to truth.

32. Through charity, you will have children, and there will be peace between them.

33. Through charity, the fruit proliferate.

34. Through charity, one draws salvation close.

35. In a time of trouble, the charity one did is remembered for him.

36. Through the charity you give, officials and kings will also have peaceful relations with you.

37. Through charity a person will not hear know from theft, armed pillage, or hunger.

38. Through charity a person merits grace.

39. One who urges people to give charity increases salvation.

Sefer HaMidot

40. When there is not someone in a city to support the needy, fire comes upon it.

41. In the merit of charity, one is saved from arrogance.

42. Faith is reckoned as charity.

43. Through charity given for the sake of Heaven, one comes to the quality of holy shame.

44. Through generosity one comes to love the tzaddikim.

45. One who steals from the poor, humiliation comes to him.

46. One who gives charity is as if he offered a sacrifice.

47. Through charity comes rain.

48. Through charity the Jews are not banished from their place.

49. When people give charity, the fruits are blessed and there is peace in the world.

50. Through truth, the charity you do is noted [lit. seen].

51. Charity protects a person's descendants.

52. One who prays for one's friend, it is reckoned for him as charity.

53. One who is materially well-off, and despite that, is miserly, literally, a bad eye, toward the poor who approach and beg him, literally, stretch out their hands, to give them; also, one who provides funding for a venture for half the profits, and they work and bring him his half, and when he sees that they are profiting and have an income and enough to suffice, he is irked by this due to his miserliness, literally,

Sefer HaMidot

bad eye, on these will be fulfilled the prophecy beginning after the verse "In the fulfillment of his needs" until "This is the portion of a wicked man."

54. One who does kindness to those who love the Blessed GOD, through this he repairs the "spoiling of the Covenant" it is a referring to sexual transgressions.

55. In the merit of the poor, we are saved from the nations.

56. When you do a mitzvah, a commandment or good deed, see to it that the mitzva is not for free, but that you pay with a full purse.

57. Due to the sin of not giving the trumah and maaser portions and tithes given to the priests, leviites, and poor, the Heavens are held up and there is strong inflation.

58. The joy one feels in giving charity is a sign of a whole heart.

59. Give charity literally do, while you still have. the opportunity; that you, found a befitting recipient, and you have the money to give, and you are still in your own hands.

60. All who give their gifts to a specific Cohen. one of the Priestly tribes. that is always favoring him and never giving the gifts to a different Cohen, bring famine to the world.

61. One who provides merchandise for Torah scholars to profit from, merits to sit in the Yeshiva of Heaven.

62. Charity is greater than all the sacrificial offerings.

63. Doing acts of kindness is greater than giving charity.

64. Lest you err and say that anyone who jumps to give charity, he is provided for, and there is produced for him

Sefer HaMidot

proper needy people, to whom to give - the Torah says, "How precious...", meaning one needs to labor and chase after them, for the proper poor they are not readily found, to merit, giving charity, with the proper poor.

65. Charity is in two areas: According to one's generosity that is when a person doesn't have very much, it is up to his generosity, and according to what God has blessed with him, that is when a person isn't generous, he should still be giving according to his wealth.

66. One who has money, but does not want to use his own money for his expenditures, so he receives from others, know that they will collect from him after his death; that he will become a slave to one from whom he took.

67. One who gives charity, even still it is possible that he will be impoverished.

68. Anyone who averts their eyes from, seeing the need to give charity, it is as if he is serving idolatry.

69. One who shears his possessions, to give charity, is saved from the judgment of Hell.

70. Even a poor person should give charity, and he will not see further signs of poverty.

Part II

1. Through sexual immorality one falls into imprisonment or diseases causing pain in the feet. Also, a student who has not reached the level of being able to rule, and rules, falls into this, also evil spirits attack [dominate] him. Charity has the segula [auspicious quality] to annul all these punishments.

2. Learning Torah, giving tithes, and keeping the Shabbat give physical life as well' that is in addition to other benefits.

Sefer HaMidot

3. Through charity, with a simple maneuver he subdues his enemies, and the Holy Blessed One saves him from grand schemes of his enemies.

4. To aid Torah scholars, with this he annuls the ruling of the stars and constellations.

5. Through those who support the poor, the masses are saved from plagues, in their merit. Also, in their merit, expanded consciousness precedes constricted consciousness.

6. Through charity, one sweetens the judgment of the Time to Come, that is, the Day of Judgment in the Time to Come. Breslovers understood the awesome import of this entry, because that future judgment will even take into account all the ramifications of that which was caused or triggered by one's deeds, our Sages revealed that even the Prophet Shmuel [Samuel] fears this judgement.

7. Those who abound in doing kindnesses, but occasionally cause something bad through their kindness, and they pretend not to see the bad that sprouted as a result of their kindness - this is an aspect of the warning to the Cohanim [the Priests], who are the aspect of kindness, that they should not take overly large steps. Through this [failing, one] causes the Judgment Above, God forbid, to be unmoderated. The same is true in the converse, when in performing kindness one is careful that bad should not result, through this the Judgment will be moderated.

8. Those who produce Torah novelty need to learn from the works of the halachic regulators before the novelty and also after, and this learning of the halachic regulators is the protection of the novelty, so that no strangers, people or forces inappropriate to such spiritual Light, touch them. Also, when one wants to give charity, it is necessary to do so - as with the novelty that is to learn halachah before and after.

Sefer HaMidot

9. Torah novelty and charity - one elicits the other.

10. Great is the power of tithing that it transforms curses to blessings.

11. Through tithes, illicit sexual thoughts are annulled.

12. One who does kindness does not need ancestral merit.

13. Through doing kindness, one gains longevity.

14. There are prayers that are not accepted Above until one gives sufficient charity, according to the number of letters in the prayer related to the problem about which one is praying. For example, when one prays the words, "Give me children", one needs to give charity according to the number of letters of "Give me children".

15. Through charity one merits to have children.

16. One who sustains the many, draws blessing from the land of Israel to the rest of the world.

17. Through money one gives to the poor of the Land of Israel, through this one merits to retain his wealth.

18. When a man moves to a city, he should send meat to the poor of that city, and through this he will find favor in the eyes of the city officials.

19. Through the giving of "shekulim", the currency used in Biblical times, one is saved from the evil inclination.

Spiritual Impurity

Part I
1. The letters Aleph-Tav-Heh א'ת'ה' subdue the evil husks.

Sefer HaMidot

2. Protection for a woman giving birth is to write on parchment the verse "Hashem, your hand was lifted up high, they did not see; they shall see and be ashamed about Your jealously for the people, the very fire for Your enemies consumes them."

3. Evil husks are found in ruins.

4. A candle subdues the dominion of the evil husks.

5. A person's good fortune protects him from being harmed.

6. The seven cries that David uttered at the water, when recited, subdue the evil spirit.

7. Damaging forces are found in pits, just like they are found in fields.

8. A place where people are not found, demons are common there even during the day. But in the city, even at night, we are not wary.

9. On the north side, demons are very much revealed to people.

10. A segula [auspicious] way to chase away the evil spirit is to recite the Torah portion of Noah.

11. When speaking with a wicked person, through the breath of his mouth we become more coarse. more physical.

Part II
1. There are demons that are found in homes which ruin peace in the home, and as a result there is anger and quarreling in the home. The mainstay of the home is the wife, because one's "house" is his wife. Therefore, in general, the quarreling mainly comes from her. Sometimes, [the demons] become attached to the other members of the home. and as a

result, they create quarreling and complaints, as [in the case of the wife]. Through this, suffering comes to the members of the household. This is explained in the verse, "Their homes are at peace from fear...". Our sages of blessed memory explained: "from fear" refers to demons. Hence, "at peace from fear": because peace is the opposite of "fear", which are the demons that ruin peace. "... and the rod of GOD is not [upon them]", referring to the aforementioned suffering.

Curse

Part I
1. Curses cause a state of mourning, GOD forbid

2. One does not have permission to curse unless he can see the generations to come from the one [he is cursing].

3. Do not take the curse of a common man lightly, in your eyes.

4. Curses affect according to the intention, with which they are said.

5. Sometimes the curse of a tzaddik are fulfilled as long as he lives, but not after his passing.

6. In the end, an unjustified curse returns upon the one who cursed.

7. The curse of a Torah sage comes to pass, even if it was unjustified, and even if it was given conditionally.

8. Even a non-Jew who blesses the Jewish People is blessed.

Part II
1. A man who is accustomed to curse is from the World of Disorder, and conversely, one accustomed to blessing is from

Sefer HaMidot

the World of Repair.

2. Investigating the World of Disorder, that is to say, speculating about what is Above and what is Below, etc., draws down curse; one who restrains himself from these investigations causes blessing.

3. One accustomed to curse through this he will not have clothes for Shabbat.

4. The power of a curse do not have effect on one with [an honored] lineage.

5. Through serving the Tzaddik comes freedom and curses are annulled.

6. Through conducting business faithfully, curses are annulled.

7. When a man curses his fellow during a time of dread, the curse is very damaging to him.

Jealousy

1. When jealousy will be annulled, the Ingathering of the Exiles will take place.

2. Through jealousy come fires burning.

3. Through jealousy comes bloodshed.

4. Through coveting the money of one's fellow, one becomes a fool.

5. Through your coming to a tzaddik, your jealousy will be annulled.

Sefer HaMidot

6. Through jealousy, one's bones rot.

7. Garlic expels jealousy.

8. One who takes revenge out of jealousy destroys his house.

9. Through jealousy comes a weakening of strength.

Nocturnal Emission

Part I

1. Nocturnal emission comes through talking about promiscuity, and also through a person falling from his faith.

2. One who intentionally releases seed wastefully, in the end goes naked.

3. Through depression, one comes to having [lit. seeing] nocturnal emission.

4. One who avoids eating food whose kashrut [kosher status] was [for what ever reason, found questionable and was deemed necessary to be] asked to an authority, he is saved from the impurity of nocturnal emission.

5. A person should not eat at the table of a tzaddik before he has immersed, in a mikva to purify himself from his emissions.

6. Rejoice in the good that comes upon the tzaddikim, and this is a rectification for emissions.

7. Through mockery, comes the impurity of nocturnal emission.

8. Nocturnal emission comes from light-headedness.

Sefer HaMidot

9. Nocturnal emission can result from eating garlic and eggs at night.

10. Also, as a result of pointless speech and foul language.

Part II

1. Drunkenness causes exile, also it causes releasing seed wastefully.

2. Ridicule comes through keri.

3. Speech that a person half-pronounces in that he does not enunciate the words clearly - this is an aspect similar to the aspect of nocturnal emissions.

4. One's children die, GOD forbid, through [lit. seeing - meaning having or experiencing] nocturnal emissions.

5. A GREAT RECTIFICATION FOR A NOCTURNAL EMISSION, GOD forbid, to say these ten chapters of Tehillim [Psalms] on the same day that it occurred to him GOD forbid, and they are [chapter numbers plus words from the beginning of the chapter]: 16 "Mikhtam liduvid", 32 "Liduvid maskil ashrei", 41 "Ashrei maskil el dul", 42 ""Ki-ayal taarohg", 59 "Lamnatzayach al tashkhais'" 77 "Al Yidusun", 90 "Tefilah liMoshe", 105 "Hodu Ladon -- oy keeroo", 137, "Al naharos Buvel", 150 "Hallilu Ail Bikudshoh" Be assured that these ten chapters are very very propitious for the rectification of this mistake, and one who is careful to say them as described above, does not need to fear anymore whatsoever, for certainly it will be rectified by this, for they are a very great rectification.

Difficulty in Childbirth

1. A woman who eats radishes while in pregnancy will have difficulties in childbirth.

Sefer HaMidot

2. A segulah for a woman having difficulty in childbirth is to give her to drink water from seven wells.

3. Also, her children should not be with her in the house.

4. Also, whisper in her ear the letters of the name Sa"g.

5. Also, her bed should not stand in the west or the south.

6. Also, hang from her neck bitter herbs left over from Passover.

7. Also, whisper to her in her ear the letters Pey - Vav - Ayin – Hey.

Vision

1. The eye can only see what it is given permission to see. Even if an object is in front him, he will not be able to see, until Heaven grants him permission to see.

2. The waning of the moon, and its eclipse, are harmful to those with weak vision.

3. Kiddush Levanah [Blessing over the New Moon] is effective [segula] for healing weak vision.

4. Saying Tikkun Chatzot, the Midnight Rectification, is effective for healing weak vision [The prayer is divided into two parts the Rectification of Rachel and the Rectification of Leah, the Bible says that Leah's eye's were worn out, so here - in Leah's rectification is a rectification for the eyes. This holds true with Rachel as well].

5. Through an oath comes pain in the eyes.

6. Hypocrites cause pain in the eyes to the masses who

are deceived by them.

7. When a great man feels some pain in his eyes, he should know that his son or his student has committed some sin.

8. One who closes his eyes to avoid seeing evil, through this he is saved from humiliation.

9. When a person goes out to the marketplace and fears he will come to [improper] thoughts through his vision - that he will see beautiful women, he should say the verse: "Hen errelum tzaaku chutza malachei shalom mar yivkuhyun, and through this he will be saved from seeing.

10. Looking at the etrog [one of the four species taken on Succos - the citrus fruit] is a healing for pain in the eyes.

11. Those with pure vision are able to see on the knives of the butchers the vessels of the Holy Temple.

12. Those with pure vision can discern in a person who his rabbi is - who taught him Torah. This is true specifically when the viewer is already familiar with the visage of the rabbi. For through the religious laws one learned from his rabbi, the face of the pupil becomes like the visage of the rabbi, for the Torah laws are his wisdom which illuminates his face, 'the wisdom of a man radiates from his face' [Kohelet - Ecclesiastes 8:1]. When the student receives the law, he receives a degree [/part] of his rabbi's visage, and the more laws he learns, the more degrees [/parts] of his visage will be accumulated.

13. Pain in the eyes is harmful at times.

14. Theft is harmful to the eyes, The Talmud Tractate Bava Kama 79b says that the theft get additional punishment for making as if the Eye of Above does not see.

Sefer HaMidot

Mercy

Part I

1. One who has mercy on the poor, merits to see the comfort of GOD, may He be blessed.

2. Also, he will always win.

3. When there is no mercy, hunger comes to the world.

4. Also, thievery increases.

5. One who prays with force merits to have mercy on the poor.

6. One who does not have mercy goes insane.

7. One who pays back good for evil, increases his length of days and years.

8. Through having mercy, your base desires are annulled.

9. When you see that your brother is in pain, and you do not help him, it is as if you did the harm.

10. One who sees his friend in pain must ask for mercy on his behalf.

11. Through asking for mercy, one merits to make marital matches which are good and honorable.

12. One who judges people favorably merits receiving the festivals appropriately.

Part II

1. Due to not asking mercy for one's friend, through this one falls into imprisonment. A repair for being imprisoned is to feed some animal.

2. Toothache comes through cruelty to animals.

3. A segula [conducive] to remove sadness - through mercy.

4. It is necessary to guard one's self from causing animals pain, for it will harm him.

Healing

1. Know, that every herb has its unique power to heal a specific sickness. However, all this is only relevant for one who did not preserve his faith, his covenant [sexual purity], and did not guard himself from transgressing "Do not disdain anyone." However, one whose faith is complete, who guards his sexual purity and is wary not transgress "Do not disdain…"- his healing is not dependent on herbs specific to his illness, rather, he can be healed by all foods and drinks, in the aspect of "and He will bless your bread," and he does not need to wait until the herbs specific to his disease are available to him.

2. Through in-depth study of the secrets of Torah, one can cause barren women to conceive and heal serious illnesses.

3. For leprosy salty things are detrimental, and its healing is fresh [naturally flowing] water. A sign for this: "The diminishing of the drops of water," that is, the leprosy that comes from the overwhelming of the blood over the water [mixed in it], through which "Yazoku- sending - rain to it's cloud". [The word Yazoku signifies damage.] [Is seems that "rain to it's cloud" is an aspect of fresh water, thus leprosy can be seen as a deficiency of fresh water - thus establishing that it can be cured by fresh water and damaged by salty things which are the anti-thesis of fresh water].

Sefer HaMidot

4. Looking at the etrog is a healing for pain in the eyes.

Oath

1. A city in which there are oaths will be ruined and destroyed, GOD forbid.

2. Through false oaths, people fall from faith.

3. Learning the Gemara tractate Shavuot [Oaths] is conducive to bring rainfall.

4. Through a false oath comes thoughts of lewdness.

5. Someone who is accustomed to making oaths, evil thoughts come to him constantly.

6. Through transgressing an oath, there is no stance in war.

7. Someone who transgresses an oath, it is certain that he does not honor the GOD fearing.

8. For all the sins in the Torah, they take retribution from him; and here - regarding oath transgressions, from him, and from his family, and from the whole world, and from him they take retribution immediately.

9. Things which even fire and water do not annihilate, false oaths annihilate them.

10. The angel Gavriel is appointed over fire, to burn and also to save.

Sabbath

1. The Torah, the tithes and the Shabbat, they give material

Sefer HaMidot

life as well.

2. One accustomed to cursing, through this he will not have appropriate clothes for the Shabbat.

3. In a city where they guard themselves from going beyond the Shabbat boundary [2000 amot beyond the last houses], through this the meat is cheap.

4. Through observing the Shabbat one draws upon oneself the light of the Messiah, also through repentance.

5. Through observing the Shabbat, one is like a son who comes clean before his father, and his father fulfills his wants. Also, he decrees, and GOD enacts. Also, the principal reward for his good deeds is preserved for the World to Come, and [in the meantime] he benefits from their dividends.

Bribery

1. A city in which bribes are accepted, armies come upon it.

2. Through bribery, one's greatness departs.

3. Through bribery come fires.

Slaughterer

1. Through morally upright shochtim people have mercy on each other, and the opposite is also true.

2. A shochet who fulfills the commandment to honor his father, the Holy One -Blessed is He - guards him from feeding people non-kosher meat, and the opposite is also true.

Sefer HaMidot

3. Due to wicked shochtim who feed - that is distribute non-kosher meat, robberies increase in the world.

4. Those with pure vision can see on the knives of the shochtim the vessels of the Holy Temple.

5. Someone who becomes suddenly mute, a kosher shochet's knife should be passed over his mouth.

Sleep

1. One who has more holiness, he is further away from sleep.

2. Through excessive sleeping and slumber, one is pushed out of the Merkava of Holiness - the chair of the Divine Presence, one's face changes, and one's GODly image is corrupted.

3. The fifteen Songs of Ascent that are in the book if Tehillim [Psalms chapters 120-134] are propitious to annul sleep.

4. One who is unable to sleep should bring to mind faith in the Resurrection.

Drunkenness

Part I
1. Through drunkenness, one falls from his level.

2. Through drinking wine, one ends up accepting bribes.

3. Drunkenness brings one to deny truth and to attest to falsehood.

4. The Holy One, Blessed be He, loves one who never gets drunk.

Sefer HaMidot

5. Oil nullifies drunkenness.

6. Vision intensifies drunkenness.

7. Through drunkenness, one falls to having promiscuous thoughts.

8. One who is drunk or a drunk, does not have the power to sweeten harsh judgments.

9. One who is drunk or a drunk, secrets of the Torah are not to be revealed to him.

10. Wine with the spice of frankincense confound a person.

Part II
1. One who is eagerly desirous to work the land, comes to one of three things; either murder, or leprosy, or drunkenness.

2. Drunkenness causes exile, and also causes spilling seed wastefully.

3. It is impossible that drunkenness will not lead to some mishap.

4. Through drunkenness, one forgets the warnings of Moshe Rabbeinu. For Moshe is enclothed in the 248 limbs of a man, and in each and every limb, he warns the man regarding the mitzvos contingent to it. Because of this Moshe is called "Mechokek" [one who engraves] the law, which has the gematria numerical value of 248.

5. Through drunkenness, one removes the kindness which clothe the daas - realization of knowledge, and clothe it with intense harshness, GOD forbid.

6. One who has enemies should swear off wine, and through this he will become their head.

Peace

1. The Shabbat candles increase peace.

2. Through pursuing peace, one merits honor in This World and life in the World to Come.

3. Anything which is for the sake of the 'ways of peace' is not subject to the injunction to "distance yourself from something false".

4. People who press [others to give] charity, through them the peace with the government increases.

5. Through pursuing peace, one comes to trust in GOD.

6. Peace comes through truth.

7. The building of Jerusalem is dependent on peace.

8. Through peace come good tidings.

9. When there is mussar [moral refinement], there is peace.

10. Through the very young school childrens studying, peace is increased.

11. Turbidity of the water is a sign that there is no peace.

12. When there is no peace, the prayers are not accepted.

13. Through peace, one merits to revelation of Eliyahu the Prophet.

14. When there is no peace, the women do not give birth to male children.

15. One who lends to people things that they need, when [a crisis causing] mass fleeing comes to the world, he will be spared.

16. Peace is a sign of life.

17. Through pursuing peace, one saves his children from death and exile.

18. Blessing comes through peace.

19. When there is peace, there is no fear.

20. Through that which there is peace among the wicked, through this, they have everything good.

21. Sometimes the Holy One, Blessed be He, makes peace among the Jewish People through evildoers.

22. Peace is an indication of satiety.

23. When the officials Above dispute with each other, immediately the same argument happens among the nations and among the scholars.

Joy

Part I
1. When a person does a mitzva joyfully, it is a sign that his heart is whole with GOD.

2. Due to joy, the heart becomes opened.

3. Through an increase in joy, the intellect is strengthened, and food and drink are powerful causes for joy in the heart,

Sefer HaMidot

and distancing sadness and worry.

4. Through giving charity with a full heart, one comes to joy.

5. Joy of performing mitzvot is strength for a man.

6. When you see that an evildoer suddenly becomes lighthearted - or laughs, it is certain that he came upon some idea to commit a sin.

7. Through the good advice that you give, you merit happiness.

8. Through the dancing and movements that you do with your body, you are aroused to joy.

9. When joy suddenly enters your heart, this is because some tzaddik has just been born.

10. Through fear comes fiery enthusiasm.

11. One who is denigrated in his own eyes comes, through this, to enthusiasm.

12. Through intentions of the heart comes joy.

13. One who is accustomed to lightheartedness, it is certain that he is far from the greatness of GOD.

14. Through music you will come to joy and enthusiasm.

15. When you give joy to the Tzaddik, you can serve GOD with joy.

16. One who publicizes the Tzaddik merits joy.

17. Through trust in GOD, one comes to joy.

Sefer HaMidot

18. Through movements of the body comes enthusiasm of the heart.

19. Through complete faith you will come to a level that you will desire, with body and soul, to serve GOD.

20. One who makes himself insignificant [lit. like leftovers] will merit enthusiasm.

21. Through joy, one's mental capacity expands.

22. Joy is a sign that a person is of stock blessed by GOD.

23. Rain falls in the merit of the joy of bride and groom.

24. Through joy of the mitzvot, GOD spreads over a person.

25. Through the joy one has on the holiday of Simchah Torah, one merits to serve GOD with love.

26. When joy comes to a person suddenly, it is certain that kindness and salvation will come to him.

27. Through joy, the honor of a person is revealed, and he also merits knowledge.

Part II
1. Someone who is always happy, through this he is successful.

2. Vows and pledges bring one to joy.

Officials

1. One who's wine is diluted with water; the officials do not deal with him in a straight manner.

Sefer HaMidot

2. One who does not judge his fellow favorably is as if he killed him. Also, the officials do not deal with him in a straight manner.

3. Saying of Hallel and giving charity are a segula [special charm] for having favor in the eyes of the minister.

4. Through eating bread baked by a non-Jew, the forest is prohibited from having its trees cut down.

5. Due to four things, the property of householders is handed over to the government or monarchy. 1. Keeping a note of debt after it has been paid off; 2. Charging interest; 3. Remaining silent in a case where one should speak out against evil; and 4. Promising to make a donation in public and not carrying through.

Chastisement

Part I

1. One who chastises must give his reproof by connecting his speech to its root, and then his admonishment will be accepted.

2. An apostate Jew, do not admonish him, for it will be of no avail.

3. Through not accepting chastisement one's home is destroyed.

4. One who chastises the world, without wisdom, through this he instigates, God forbid, great exile and pressure from the nations.

5. A person should never exclude himself from the collective - group of Jews.

Sefer HaMidot

6. Due to punishment for a lack of chastisement, GOD retracts from the good He had said - He would bring.

7. When you know that people will not accept chastisement, let them be.

8. One who is fearful of people to chastise them, in the end GOD breaks him in front of them.

9. Someone who is in a position to warn and does not warn, is also held accountable for the downfall [literally - blood] of his friend.

10. Through giving charity, one merits to receive mussar [ethical criticism].

11. One who does not accept mussar [ethical criticism] is sentenced to death.

12. Through the chastisement you give, you merit to rest in the grave without the pains of Hell, and you will merit to the Garden of Eden.

13. It is permitted to push away with both hands, one who did not accept chastisement from you.

14. As long as there is chastisement in the world, satisfaction, good, and blessing come to the world.

15. Through chastisement, judgments are sweetened, and kindness is drawn.

Part II
1. One who has not reached a high level of righteousness, and does not have ancestral merit, yet wants to draw people to the service of GOD, should guard himself from tests, especially that the wicked should not envy him.

Sefer HaMidot

2. One who draws close those who are far, to the service of the Blessed Lord, the blessings are given over to his hands - that is he is empowered to grant blessings.

3. One who hears chastisement and does not accept it, should know that he will need to borrow from others. A sign for this is: "A slave will not be corrected by words", and "A borrower is a slave to the one who lent him".

4. No one is able to throw words into the mouth of his friend from a distance - a concept found in the Medrash on the verse, that GOD shot His words into Moshe's mouth. Not until he brings his friend first into the aspect of "fetus", that is, a state of spiritual renewal. This can be derived from the above noted verse, where God says he will "teach" Moshe what to say, and the Medrash offers to additional meanings for the word "teach": shooting - hence the first part of this dictum; and the second, to become pregnant with - hence the contingency of the second part of the dictum.

5. With this, that people go out to greet an important man, the ten statements with which the world was created, are aroused. This is done also through drawing the far, close [to GOD].

Prayer

Part I

1. A person should yearn and long for the general good, even though it will draw for himself alone, a loss.

2. One who prays in a synagogue, it is as if he brings a pure meal offering - mincha.

3. The Holy One, Blessed be He, is found in the synagogue.

4. Due to adulation, one's prayer is not heard.

Sefer HaMidot

5. Through engaging in Torah whilst under duress, one's prayer is heard.

6. One who prays for his friend, and he himself needs the thing he is praying for he is answered first.

7. One who has a humble opinion of himself, his prayer is not despised.

8. A person should always preempt prayer before trouble.

9. Anyone who exerts himself in prayer below, enemies are not able to oppose him above.

10. A person should always beseech mercy, that everyone strengthens him, and that the ministering angels assist him in requesting mercy, and that they or there should not oppose him from above.

11. The prayer of another is more effective than one's own prayer, and even a tzaddik needs the prayers of others.

12. It is permissible to pray regarding a habitual slanderer, that he should die, and that his Torah be forgotten, and that he should not have a portion in the World to Come, and that he should not have wise children.

13. Anyone who engages in Torah, the Holy One, Blessed be He, fulfills his needs.

14. Crying out is good for a person, whether before the decree or after the decree.

15. A person should not beseech excessively for anything.

16. On a rainy day, salvation flourishes in the world, and advocates of merit enter before Him [GOD].

Sefer HaMidot

17. The prayer of an individual is not heard unless he concentrates in his heart, but the prayer of a congregation is heard, even though all of them do not [pray with] a full heart.

18. One should not pray for two things at once.

19. It is forbidden to burden Hashem to change nature.

20. One who is forbearing, his prayer is heard.

21. One who excessively relates the praises of the Omnipresent One is uprooted from the world.

22. A synagogue in which financial calculations are made - in the end, the body of a met mitzvah - an anonymous corpse whose duty of burial falls on the congregation at large, will repose there.

23. Every matter of holiness requires preparation and invitation, this is done by reciting a short disclosure beforehand stating and praying that one's intent to do such and such a mitzva will be for the sake of unifying the Name of GOD, and at this time one should also bind one's self to the tzadikim.

24. In requesting one's needs, one should not be so bold [lit. raise one's head] as to ask for a huge request. However, in matters of Torah and fear of Heaven, one should request all that he desires.

25. It is a mitzva for one to have respectable clothing at the time of prayer.

26. They instituted blessings to GOD in This World, so that people should become accustomed - to saying them, in the World to Come.

27. A person should ask for mercy, that he not come to

poverty.

28. Through prayer, one can change the fortunes, set by the constellations.

29. Speaking in a loud voice brings feeling and movement to all the limbs.

30. One who is moved in his spirit to plead before Hashem, may He be Blessed, through this he finds grace in the eyes of Hashem, may He be Blessed.

31. Through having trust, the Holy One, Blessed be He, hears one's prayers.

32. Do not pray in a house built by a conflict monger.

33. Before the prayer, give charity, and bind yourself to the tzaddikim of the generation [this is done with a verbal disclosure, "I hereby bind myself to all the true tzadikim of the generation, and to all the true tzadikim who dwell in the earth, holy ones who are in the ground, and especially to our holy master, the tzadik foundation of the world, gushing river source of wisdom. And my mouth is as theirs, and all my thoughts and intentions are as theirs, and it should be desirable before the Master of All" - and in this way one should pray feeling the presence of the tzadikim praying with him.

34. A person receives abundance and GODly power according to the place where he prays.

35. When a congregation prays, it is a time of Divine favor.

36. One who has access to a synagogue, and does not enter there to pray, causes his children to be exiled.

37. For everything - whether for something big, or for

something small - you should pray.

38. Come early and stay late in the synagogue, for this is how you will lengthen your life.

39. One who has the ability to beseech mercy for his friend, and does beseech, is called a inadvertent sinner.

40. One who relieves himself, washes his hands, dons tefillin, recites the Shema and prays, it is as if he built an altar and offered a sacrifice on it, and it is as if he ritually immersed.

41. One who is careful not to say words of holiness in a filthy house - a place where due to the filth Jewish law forbids speaking holy words, will merit length of days.

42. Prayer is greater than good deeds and sacrifices.

43. Torah, good deeds, prayer, and good manners require encouragement.

44. Only pray in house that has windows.

45. Through giving charity with two hands, one's prayer is heard.

46. During prayer, one should spread out one's hands or palms, as if he is receiving something.

47. Due to stealing, or embarrassing one's fellow man, one's prayer is not heard.

48. Shabbat and Rosh Chodesh [the first of the Jewish month] are more conducive [segula] to bring up the prayer.

49. When a person is constipated, this is a sign that his prayer is not accepted.

Sefer HaMidot

50. Through the longing that a person longs at night for Hashem, may He be Blessed, through this it is easy for him to pray in the morning.

51. Prayer which is tearful, it is accepted.

52. When you pray for something, you should mention ancestral merit.

53. When the Holy One, Blessed be He, punishes an evildoer that He knows will not ever repent, and the Tzaddik prays too much for him, through this the Tzaddik is punished.

54. When someone praying falls into small-mindedness, this is a sign that his prayer will not be accepted - the original text has a noted mistake - confused.

55. When you are not at peace with the world, your prayer is not accepted.

56. You should pray for the peace of the city in which you live.

57. Someone who prays joyfully, the Holy One, Blessed be He, honors him and punishes his oppressors.

58. Through saying Tikkun Chatzot [the Midnight Rectification], one reminds the Holy One, Blessed be He, of the favors He promised to do for Israel.

59. One who educes merit of Israel especially where circumstances would seemingly deem the culpable, through this, he arouses salvation, and the salvation comes through his hand.

60. One who does not pray concerning the suffering of Israel is called a inadvertent sinner.

Sefer HaMidot

61. A person needs to pray for his offspring, and for all those who will come after him.

62. It is forbidden for a person to be ungrateful, neither to a Jew nor to a Gentile.

63. Someone who prays on for the sake of Israel, the Holy One, Blessed be He, atones for all his sins.

64. A sick person who prays for himself with tears, the Holy One, Blessed be He, will certainly heal him and accept his prayers.

65. When you want to uplift your prayer, pray for the sake of Israel.

66. The Holy One, Blessed be He, requests of a person to pray before Him.

67. Someone who saves a poor person from someone physically stronger than him, koach - strength, power, conviction - perhaps also an allusion to the 28 letters of creation. is easily in the letters of the prayer.

68. Through having trust in GOD, a person's prayer is heard.

69. Someone who is humble is able to cry out in his prayer from the heart.

70. Through joy, your prayer will come into the palace or chamber of the King.

71. One who derives no pleasure from his prayer, should pray with glad song.

72. One who prays with intensity, the Holy One, Blessed be He, hears his prayer.

Sefer HaMidot

73. One who took a vow upon himself, his prayer is not accepted until he fulfills his vow.

74. One who does not have faith, his prayer is not heard.

75. One who makes the tzadik happy, is prayer is heard.

76. Before praying, one should attach one's spirit to the Creator, and due to the attachment, the words will emerge from his mouth of their own accord.

77. When you hear yourself being humiliated and you are silent, you merit that the Holy One, Blessed be He, will answer your request.

78. One who prays for his friend, through this the Holy One, Blessed be He, doubles for him the good he receives.

79. Prayer that is not accepted above is burned.

80. One who prays about the destruction of the Temple, through this, he will merit to pray with heart and body.

81. Prayer done with joy is pleasing and sweet to Hashem, may He be Blessed.

82. One who has humility - even when he prays only in thought, the Holy One, Blessed be He, fulfills his thought.

83. Sometimes, the Holy One, Blessed be He, does not accept the prayer of a tzaddik when he prays for some person. For the Holy One, Blessed be He, knows that in the course of time, this man will draw the tzaddik into the some of the sins that he himself commits.

84. Thoughts only follow after one who is serving. [Explanation: One who serves Hashem, thoughts follow and are drawn after him, to confuse him more than other people.

Sefer HaMidot

And this is: "Thoughts only follow after one who serves".] [The above explanation is found in the original text. This explanation actually takes the adage out of the simple context which is a Talmudic ruling regarding the offering of a sacrifice which needs certain purity of thought, and there is question as to whose thoughts can effect the sacrifice].

Part II

1. Due to not asking mercy upon one's friend, one falls into incarceration. The rectification for incarceration - that he should provide for animals.

2. Prayer is paramount [another text: is effective] when one's face is turned upward.

3. One who requests mercy for the members of his generation merits revelation of the Divine Presence.

4. Through songs and praises, one draws down the Divine Presence.

5. The prayer of the leader of the prayer service possesses the aspect of war.

6. One who fulfills the maxim "Your fellow man's money should be as dear to you as your own", through this he merits to pray with heartfelt intention.

7. The saying of Tehilim [Psalms of kink David] is conducive [segula] to causing rain to fall. This is learned from the Hebrew letters of the word.

8. Anyone who is troubled by the sufferings of the Israel and prays for them, even though he slams his words [slightly disrespectfully] towards Heaven, he is not punished.

9. There are prayers that are not accepted Above until one gives the amount of charity equal to the number of letters in

Sefer HaMidot

the prayer relevant to the matter. For example, when one prays with the words "Give me children", one needs to give charity according to the number of the letters in the words "Give me children" [The number of the levels probably means the gematria- numerical value - in the example given this would be 592, in Hebrew letters this would spell out the word - you give the set amount].

10. Through prayer, one can change the marital match proclaimed for him in Heaven.

11. The prayers of the many are heard more when they are gathered together, then to when they are scattered about.

12. Sometimes salvation does not come until several people pray, and the prayer of an individual is not enough.

13. One who has enemies, it is difficult for him to concentrate in prayer.

14. One must be careful when one mentions the Name of GOD, that it be said in holiness and purity. That is, he should sanctify the breath of his mouth to such a degree that it becomes the aspect of the spirit of prophecy. Then, this spirit goes out and casts down those who trust in falsehood and vanity. This is [hinted at in the first letters of the verse] BShem"Y'KVK'A'elokainu'N'azkir ["With the Name of the Lord our GOD we mention"] [NAB'Y Prophet. And the next verse continues:] "They bowed and fell."

Repentance

Part I
1. Fasting helps for everything.

2. One who is bereft of any good deeds cannot separate others from their evil.

Sefer HaMidot

3. A fast is stronger than a sword.

4. It is fitting that repentance should be done through the very same matter [wherein one sinned].

5. When a person thinks, 'I will do such and such; such and such I will attain', through this his thought is not fulfilled.

6. Exile atones for everything.

7. One who is humble, it is as if he offered all the sacrifices.

8. Anyone who confesses has a portion in the World to Come.

9. One who teaches his friend's son Torah is as if he created him, and as if he made the words of Torah, and as if he made himself.

10. Rav [Rabbi] Papa fasted for having referred to a Torah scholar in a disparaging fashion.

11. A person should guard his mouth from saying, "I will do such and such a sin", even mockingly, for his words force him to do the action.

12. Anyone who cries in the night, his cries are heard, and the stars and the constellations cry with him.

13. Those liable to kurais [lit. cut off - this is a Divine punishment of early death] who received lashes, they are absolved from kurais.

14. When suffering comes to the world, one should think it is because of his sins that this suffering came.

15. The clothes that are made for the Tzaddik - each garment has its own unique segula [power] to atone.

Sefer HaMidot

16. When [lit. since or because] a man marries a woman, all his sins are forgiven [literally, sealed off].

17. When one sees or hears about some suffering that befell a non-Jew, he should have thoughts of repentance.

18. One who lives in Israel fares without sin.

19. It is appropriate to lighten the conditions of repentance on the sinners.

20. Sin weakens the strength of a man.

21. When two mitzvos – commandments or good deeds come to your hands, do that mitzva that demands greater restraint of your desires.

22. It is necessary to fast when causing suffering to the Tzaddik.

23. Pain in the heart is close to shedding tears.

24. One who brings others back in repentance merits to sit in the Yeshiva Above, and the Holy One, Blessed is He, annuls a harsh decree for him.

25. A person's despondence is greater than a fast.

26. One who does a sin and then regrets it, all his sins are forgiven.

27. One who does business dealings faithfully, all his sins are forgiven.

28. The first thoughts help a person through the execution and finishing of the project, that it should be carried out in holiness. However, if he did not think in holiness at the beginning, then mishaps will arise in the middle and at the end.

29. **A** table to which guests are invited atones.

30. Greatness atones.

31. Sometimes when a person starts to repent, sufferings come upon him. This is because he delayed repenting.

32. Through the sigh that that is sighed, one becomes a new being.

33. Through having love for the tzaddikim, the tzaddikim are able to bring the people back in repentance.

34. One who brings back the people in repentance, in his merit there is no fear and contention in the world.

35. One who helps orphans, subdues [lit. breaks] the power of the nations through this, and through their being subdued [lit. broken], the wicked of the Jews return in repentance.

36. One who brings people back in repentance is saved from jail.

37. Also, he is honorable in GOD's eyes.

38. Also, he merits becoming famous among the nations.

39. One who's way is to constantly bring people back in repentance, in his merit foreign thoughts desist from the leaders [lit. great] of the generation.

40. One who brings back evildoers in repentance will merit to observe [lit. guard] the Shabbat.

41. Also, he will not be harmed from a snake.

Sefer HaMidot

42. When you teach the son of a wicked person the good way and proper conduct, through this you will be able to annul harsh decrees.

43. Through falsehood one strengthens the hands of the wicked.

44. One who repents with all his heart, the Holy One - Blessed is He - gives him a heart to know Him.

45. Through hearing the shofar blown by an upright [lit. kosher] man, the evil inclination is broken, and repentance is aroused in the world.

46. One who wants to repent should take precation of being in debt.

47. One who loves the tzaddikim is able to bring people back in repentance.

48. One who confesses, the Holy One - Blessed is He - loves him with a munificent love, and withdraws His anger from him.

49. The nations are close to repentance.

50. Learning the Torah atones.

51. One who is on a high level can reach his perfection with a minimum of actions.

52. When some suffering comes upon you, examine your deeds.

53. One who wants to do good deeds but is prevented with impediments, the Holy One - Blessed He- rewards him as if he had done them. But one who does not do as much as he could, he receives punishment for this.

Sefer HaMidot

54. One who causes the people to gain merit becomes a partner with GOD in the Creation of the World.

55. There is no comparison between a mitzva commandment and good deed, one does for himself alone, even if it be great, to a mitzva which will bring merit to the people, even if it be small.

56. The demand to earn a living, and enemies, and disease, and overabundant wealth prevent a man from reaching perfection and the ultimate purpose.

57. When you do some damage, it is a sign that the evil inclination dominates over you.

58. One who tempts his fellowman away from the good path, fire [lit. burning] comes upon him.

59. One who is unable to cry, the segula [propitious] for this is - he should sit in a place where two rivers pour out together.

60. One who returns people back in repentance merits wisdom.

61. Through laziness, it appears to a person that the way of repentance is hidden from him.

62. One who reveals his secrets, it becomes hard for the thing, he revealed, to endure, or be fulfilled.

63. One who is ashamed of his sins, the Holy One - Blessed is He- deals with him charitably.

64. A fast that is without cognizance is not considered a fast.

65. From the moment a person thinks of repenting, his prayers are accepted, even if he has not yet actually repented.

Sefer HaMidot

66. When you want to repent, ask the Tzaddik to bring you before the Blessed GOD.

67. Through kindness and truth, sins are forgiven.

68. Through your asking GOD to give you love, GOD covers over your sins.

69. One who confesses his sins will merit that he will not have to sell from the inheritance or estates of his forefathers.

70. When you chastise those, who have not corrected the sins of their youth, include yourself with them, and through this they will accept from you.

71. The main rectification for the blemish from one's sins is through submission.

72. A person should rebuke himself every morning.

73. The service with which a man serves GOD in his youth, every day of service - its value is much greater than many years of serving GOD in his old age.

74. It is impossible for a man to know in his lifetime, if his repentance was accepted, Even though the actual repentance has to be strong enough that even GOD guarantees that he will not repeat the offense again, that still doesn't guarantee that it was accepted.

75. That which we see, that someone who begins to serve GOD, suffering comes upon him, this is because he began with fear of justice.

76. One who starts to serve GOD, the Holy One - Blessed is He- says to him, "I know that your longing and desire is to serve Me. But what assurance do I have that tomorrow you will not leave me? So how can I draw you close for the wish you desire, and how can I reveal to you hidden things right away? Rather do the following: In the beginning, love Me this way and do my commandments, even though you do not know the reason [lit. intellect] of the mitzva, and serve Me simply without sophistication. When you serve Me this way for a long time [lit. many times], I will believe you, and reveal to you the reason and the intellect of every matter, and I will draw you close with every form of bonding. For the long period that you served Me beforehand, is assurance that you will not desert Me."

77. Through this a person can know if he truly wants to serve GOD - when he has no interest in his own renown.

78. One who does not know the Way of GOD should belittle himself.

79. Through prayer that is expressed intensely [Raised voice and uplifted eyes - Zohar], GOD will forgive you.

80. Due to falsehoods, a person cannot improve his behavior.

81. One who cannot annul his evil inclination through drawing it to the hall of study should know that he is still in a state of wickedness.

82. The Holy One - Blessed is He- desires the mitzvos in which a person also does the will of people, more than those mitzvos which are matters between man and his Creator.

83. It is better for a person to fulfill the mitzva however much possible, than to abandon it altogether.

84. Repairing the body comes before repairing the soul.

85. One who cries and mourns over a kosher man is forgiven for all his sins.

Sefer HaMidot

86. It is a mitzva to cause people to repent [alternate text: to warn people] regarding every sin. If you fear that they will not listen to you, say your words in the name of a different tzaddik, so that they will listen to you.

87. All who say Vayechulu - which is customarily said as part of the prayers on the Shabbat night, with intention, and pray with intention, the Ministering Angels ask GOD to forgive them.

88. One who answers Amen Yehey Shmey Rabah - This is a response in the Kadish, where the chazon, leader of the service, says. The great name of GOD should be aggrandized and sanctified, in the world that He created as He willed, and His monarchy should be established.... To this proclamation everyone responds: Amen, the great Name should be greatly blessed forever and ever] with all his might - even if he has a smudge of idol worship, he is forgiven.

89. The following do not see the face and presence of Hell: Those in extreme poverty, and those with stomach illness, and someone who has creditors, and someone who has burden or pressure or persecution, of the sovereignty.

90. Strengthen yourself in doing mitzvos, beyond what is in your power to do.

91. Monetary loss atones for one's body.

92. Thirst is a rectification for unnecessary speech.

93. Repentance brings healing to the world.

94. By doing repentance out of fear, one's deliberate sins become as if they were inadvertent. By repenting out of love, they become like merits.

95. Repentance brings close the Redemption, and lengthens

Sefer HaMidot

the days and the years of a man.

96. Through repentance of an individual, he is forgiven, and the whole entire world.

97. The Holy One - Blessed is He- is pacified by confession, and the one who confesses, is as if he built an altar and offered a sacrifice.

98. One who is resilient in how people treat him, GOD overlooks all his sins.

99. The learning of Torah and doing acts of kindness atone.

100. Crying out and weeping in the night has more influence in arousing mercy - Elsewhere we learn that the arousal of mercy should be undertaken only in the second half of the night.

101. A ba'al tshuvah [someone who has returned in repentance] should pray for rain, and through this all his sins are atoned.

102. When the Jewish People fast, they are not answered until evildoers are included in the union.

103. The path a person should select is to love rebuke - given to him, and to hold himself in or to more or extra faith.

Part II
1. The day that a person repents is beyond [lit. above] time, and it raises all the days beyond [lit. above] time, and so, Yom Kippur is beyond [lit. above] time.

2. Also, through repentance, the Spirit of Messiah whisks upon the decrees of the nations [lit. kingdoms] and annuls them.

Sefer HaMidot

3. Also, through repentance, great heat is annulled.

4. The young are easier to return to the Blessed GOD than the elderly.

5. One must force the wicked with monetary pressure so that they return in repentance.

6. Through repentance, livelihood comes easily.

7. Through the exceptionally brilliant and sharp of the generation, awe is aroused [lit. illuminated], and through the awe, the merit of the forefathers is kindled [lit. sparks or sparkles], and through the sparkling of the forefathers, repentance is aroused in the world.

8. The Holy One, Blessed is He- creates paths in the sea, in order to overpower our sins and to extract our righteousness.

9. When the Tzaddik becomes wealthy, through this the wicked return in repentance.

10. Through observing the Shabbat, one draws on oneself the light of the Messiah, also through repentance.

www.ingramcontent.com/pod-product-compliance
Lightning Source LLC
Chambersburg PA
CBHW070132080526
44586CB00015B/1654